BOWLING

BEING THE PRACTICE OF THE ANCIENT &
ROYAL GAME OF BOWLS

BY

JAMES A. MANSON
("JACK HIGH")

WITH EIGHT DIAGRAMS IN THE TEXT

A. & C. BLACK LTD.
4, 5 & 6 SOHO SQUARE, LONDON, W. 1
1923

CONTENTS

CHAPTER I

The Wearing of the Green

Bowls as a Christmas Sport—A Contractor Essential—The Ideal Green—The Ditchboard Inquiry—Solway Turf—Drawbacks of Small Greens—Weeds—The Kew Lawns—Worms—Darwin's View—Daniel Leslie's Treatment—Climate and Greens—Scythe, Lawn-mower, and Roller—"Tricky" Greens—How Bias may be Nullified—The Old English Bowl—The Crown-Green Game—The Groundman—One Green One Man—The Greenkeeper in Winter—Tippling, Tipping, and Tobacco—The Ranger, or Green Rota—Loan of Rinks, or Green—The Golden Rule 1

CHAPTER II

The Flowing Bowl

"Bools and the Man"—The Stone Age—The Age of Wood—Excelite—What is a Bowl?—What is Bias?—Loading with Lead—Messrs. Barclay & Perkins's Tudor Bowls—*Lignum Vitæ*—The Making of a Bowl—The Turner's Art—The "Eyes," or Ivories—The Testing-Room—Varnished—Veining of the Wood—Weight of the Bowls—Bowls in Ronuk—Too Narrow Bias—The English B.A. and Bias—What *is* a Standard Bowl's Bias?—The Proper Bias—Undersized Bowls 24

CONTENTS

CHAPTER III

The Rudiments

BUYING BOWLS—SWEAR WORDS—THROWING THE JACK—Winning the Toss—Defects of the Scots Law—The English Practice—That an Unstraightened Jack is Playable—Various Names for the Jack—BIAS IN ACTION—Forehand and Backhand Play—"Visualise the Track of your Bowl!"—Wrong Bias—Cultivate Play on Both Hands—STYLE AND ATTITUDE—Different Attitudes Considered—DELIVERING THE BOWL—Throwing and Dumping—The Right Mode of Delivery—Playing on a Soft Green—How to Hold the Bowl—"Be Up!" and "Take Green!" 34

CHAPTER IV

The Rink Game

The Word "Rink"—The Quartet of Players—He who Must be Obeyed—Discipline and Combination—THE LEADER—THE SECOND PLAYER—Card of the Match—THE THIRD MAN—THE SKIP—Knowledge of Human Nature—The Unsuitable Man—"What Do you See?"—Discreet Praise of his Men—The Noisy Skip—The Policy of Firing—Carrying the Jack—The Question of Guarding—Watch the Measure—Win Well and Lose Well—"Touchers"—Spat upon *Honoris Causa*—"Ditchers"—The "Live Jack"—The English Practice Preferable—The Captain 59

CHAPTER V

The Points Game and Fixed Jack

Playing with the Head—Infinite Variety in Bowls—THE GAME OF POINTS—Preparation of the Green—Rules of the Competition—DRAWING—Disposition of the

CONTENTS

Plan—GUARDING—Arranging the Ground—TRAILING—The Prepared Green—DRIVING—To Encourage Proficiency in Drawing—FIXED JACK—Plan of the Green—Duties of the Starter—The Marker and the Score—The Carried Jack—Line Bowls—Method of Play 78

CHAPTER VI

THE LAWS OF BOWLS

The Twenty Laws of the Game—I. Rinks, or Divisions of the Green—II. Bowls : Size and Bias—III. Size of the Jack—IV. Conditions of a Game—V. Rink, or Team of Players—VI. Skips, or Drivers—VII. The Mat—VIII. Throwing the Jack—IX. Movement of the Jack and of Bowls—X. Jack, or Bowl Rebounding—XI. Jack, or Bowl Burned—XII. Touchers—XIII. Ditchers—XIV. Possession of the Rink—XV. Result of Head—XVI. Changing Bowls—XVII. Objects on the Green—XVIII. Leaving the Green—XIX. Single-handed Games—XX. Onlookers 94

APPENDIX—International Results 113

INDEX 117

DIAGRAMS

	PAGE
THE UNSTRAIGHTENED JACK	43
BIAS ACTING NORMALLY	48
WRONG BIAS	49
HEAD SET FOR DRAWING	81
HEAD ARRANGED FOR GUARDING	83
HEAD PREPARED FOR TRAILING	85
HEAD MADE READY FOR DRIVING	86
FIXED JACK : GREEN SET FOR TWELVE JACKS .	90–91

CHAPTER I

THE WEARING OF THE GREEN

Bowls as a Christmas Sport—A Contractor Essential—The Ideal Green—The Ditchboard Inquiry—Solway Turf—Drawbacks of Small Greens—Weeds—The Kew Lawns—Worms—Darwin's View—Daniel Leslie's Treatment—Climate and Greens—Scythe, Lawn-mower, and Roller—"Tricky" Greens—How Bias may be Nullified—The Old English Bowl — The Crown-Green Game — The Groundman—One Green One Man—The Greenkeeper in Winter—Tippling, Tipping, and Tobacco—The Ranger, or Green Rota—Loan of Rinks, or Green—The Golden Rule.

"WHANNE that April with his showres sote [sweet] the draughte of March hath percèd to the rote [root]," the Bowler begins to examine with anxious heed the condition of his green, for he hopes to renew acquaintance with the turf on " the maddest, merriest day " of all the year, or on the first Saturday of May.

Bowls in the open air in winter is not unknown, but may be looked at in the light of a freak of Sport. During a spell of " by-ordinar' " geniality, the greenkeeper of the Alloa West End B.C., finding the turf in fit order, trimmed and rolled the green, and

I

invitations were promptly issued for a match between the West End and East End Clubs of the town on January 3rd, 1911. Play lasted for more than two hours, and all the time the sun shone brilliantly on a " dour fecht," for the home team only won by seven shots (71-64). Yet on the very same day curlers enjoyed the " roaring game " on the artificial pond in Alloa Park !

Further, Dr. Robert Carruthers tells us that, towards the end of the 18th century, Christmas festivities in Inverness " were usually kept up for two or three weeks—the gentlemen playing Bowls during the day, and the ladies amusing themselves at the card tables." W. W. Mitchell, when in his seventy-seventh year, played for four hours on Christmas Day, 1879, on one of the Willowbank greens in Glasgow, " as well, perhaps, as ever he had previously done," the turf being protected by a sheet of oilcloth, about six feet long, to receive the take-off of the bowls.

But, such exceptions notwithstanding, it is reasonable to paraphrase what old Tom Morris said of golf courses, when asked what he thought about Sunday play, " If Bowlers don't need a rest, the green does." Upon a perfect green Bowls is quite another game from what it is upon a lawn of common or meadow turf. Then even the tyro will discover the unsuspected

A CLUB'S FIRST DUTY

beauties of the game, while the veteran never wearies of trying for fresh varieties of defence and attack—the gambits of Bowls. In short, the difference between a perfect green and a third- or fourth-rate one measures the difference between a game of skill and a game largely of luck.

What, then, is the whole duty of a Bowling Club, starting *de novo* ? In the first place, it must take care that the ground it is about to acquire is large enough to allow of (*a*) the construction of a full-sized green, with surrounding pathway and flower-beds, and (*b*) the erection of a pavilion, bowl-house, and lavatory, and (*c*), if possible, a lawn for croquet or tennis. (This last is an " extra " that will be appreciated by the ladies, who are so good as to preside over Saturday teas and other social functions.) The moving spirits will, of course, " raise the wind " before proceeding with their undertaking, the cost of which can be exactly ascertained before a single document is signed. In view of the expense it is clear that the lease should be for a long period—not less than twenty-one years.

In the second place, it is extremely desirable that the promoters should engage a professional contractor of repute to construct the green and its surroundings, leaving the pavilion to be erected by a local builder. If the founders cannot draw up a full specification, it will be in order to ask the contractor to submit one, *with inclusive charges*, and, as a matter of business, it is usual to approach two or three contractors, so as to compare and check prices, and so forth. As a rule, the contractor will inspect the ground before tendering, and the promoters may then elicit all the information they wish for.

To prevent misapprehension, the projectors must understand that an ideal green is 42 yards square, but that, in addition, there will be required all round the green ground for the ditch (14 inches wide), the banks (18 inches wide), the pathway (at least six feet), and the flower-bed beyond (say, 12 feet). Therefore for the green and its surroundings, independently of space for the pavilion and adjuncts, and the croquet or tennis lawn, an area at least 50 yards square should be reserved, and even with this allowance things may be a little cramped. Where land is plentiful, 70 yards square, or the equivalent of an acre, would provide a splendid pitch.

It should be explained that the dimensions of a green are not governed by the laws of the game, save by inference. In cricket, for example, the M.C.C. enactments stipulate that the stumps shall be pitched 22 yards apart, neither more nor less; but in Bowls a certain

THE IDEAL GREEN

degree of latitude is sanctioned. The first law enjoins that a rink, or playing space, shall be not less than 19 feet, nor more than 21 feet wide; and the eighth law requires the jack to be thrown not less than 25 yards from the mat, while it may be thrown as much farther as the player pleases, provided that, when it comes to rest, it shall be at least six feet from the ditch. Subject, therefore, to these imperative conditions the size of the green may be regarded as an open question.

In actual experience, however, it has been found—as we have just said—that a green 42 yards square furnishes an ideal lawn. There are substantial reasons for this preference. A green of that size admits of six rinks (21 feet × 6 = 126 feet, or 42 yards), affording space for forty-eight players, that is, eight players (four a-side) to every rink. This would supply ample accommodation for a club of one hundred members at least, and it is by no means uncommon, on holidays and even of a Saturday afternoon, when there is a large muster of members, for seven rinks to be in full swing at once on a green 42 yards square. In these friendly games such infringement of the letter of the law is winked at as innocent, though it would be improper in matches and handicaps.

But there is another consideration of, at all

events, equal importance in constructing a green 42 yards square, in that it allows of play in opposite directions in alternate weeks. Suppose, by way of illustration, that play is had one week from north to south and south to north, in the following week it would be made from east to west and west to east; such an arrangement is of inestimable benefit to the green, which is thus rested in both directions in turns every other week. It is customary to find a scientifically-laid green exhibiting scarcely any signs of wear and tear at the close of the busiest season. I examined the Lutton Place green one autumn, and was astonished to discover not the slightest trace of weakness, and this must be one of the hardest-worked greens in Scotland.

If is safe to say that in Scotland not a green can be seen without a ditch, and it is equally safe to say that, until 1871, or thereabouts, in England south of the Border counties not a green could have been seen with one. The " toucher " game renders a ditch essential, and, since it plays a prominent part in nearly every end, it is important to keep the ditch in good order. In 1908 the Scottish B.A. undertook a " ditchboard inquiry " which was of some practical value. In order that " touchers " driven into the ditch might come to rest as near as possible to the spot where they entered

CONCERNING THE DITCH

it, the Scots Council advised constituent clubs to see that the boards, or cross-spars bottoming the ditch, were not less than two inches and a half below the surface of the green. This recommendation not having been complied with generally, the question next arose whether gravel, or sand, or other suitable material should not be substituted for ditch-boards, and the clubs were requested to report whether their greens were equipped with ditch-boards, or with ditches containing gravel or sand. Only some 40 per cent. of the clubs chose to respond, and it appeared that seventy-four used ditchboards (that is to say, kept the ditches empty), forty-three gravel, twenty-three sand, while ten used other materials. Having regard to the comparative indifference with which many clubs viewed the subject and the wide variety of usage evidenced by the practice of the clubs that had reported, the Scottish B.A. did not feel empowered to take legislative action.

Gravel or sand promptly stops the career of driving or driven bowls, and either substance, in this respect, is superior to the wooden spars of the ditchboard. On the other hand, a ditch full of small gravel is a permanent nuisance, and the ends of many a beautiful green are disfigured by stray pebbles kicked or knocked out of the ditch. Sea sand, well sifted before being deposited in the ditch, is so far free from objection that its presence on the green is not detrimental either to the turf or a bowl on the draw.

Most new greens are laid with turf from the Solway Firth, much of the sward lying within tidal limits. Every effort should be made to enable the contractor to lay the green in autumn, so that the turf may have a chance of establishing itself before frost sets in. Naturally members expect to enjoy a full season's play, and this will only be possible on a green that has been finished not later than the previous November. When a contractor pooh-poohs this, it is likely he has an interest in postponing operations until after Christmas. Play may be had in May on a new green completed in November, but it would be foolish to play before July on a green finished in February. The objection to allowing a green to lie fallow for a whole season is that, in such circumstances, it would be difficult, if not impossible, to keep the club together. This course, however, can be adopted in the case of a club which is obliged to leave its old quarters and which, taking time by the forelock, lays its new green during the last season of play on the old one.

In country towns ground for a full-sized green should be obtainable easily enough, but

MAKESHIFT GREENS

in London and other populous centres, where land is dear and not always available, clubs have sometimes to be content with the largest space they can get. Usually they can always secure an area that will furnish room for a fair-length jack and three rinks. But such a green cannot be played upon up and down one week and crosswise the next, and so on alternately, because the total width (say, 24 yards) clearly will not allow of even a minimum jack. Accordingly play can only be had in one direction (to and fro). Moreover, if the green be also deficient in length, both ends of the lawn are sure to be worn " to the bone " before the close of the season. Though remote from the ideal, such a green is quite a possible green; in fact, a lawn only big enough for one rink, but 10 yards wide and 35 yards long, would yet be a green within " the meaning of the Act." But every green of distinctly limited dimensions is a standing worry. For one thing, the ends must be re-laid every autumn, and repair on this humble scale must necessarily be undertaken by the groundman, who may or may not make a good job of it. Hence excess of zeal in prolonging the season in the event of a mild October is mischievous, since it postpones the inevitable repair.

In addition to renewal of turf, the green should also be weeded. Hand weeding is the safest way to eradicate weeds, but the careful labour this demands can seldom be procured. Consequently various chemicals are resorted to, but they must not be indiscriminately employed. For charlock, daisies, plantains, and other rough-leaved weeds, it is stated that copper sulphate (in the proportion of forty gallons of a 4 per cent. solution to the acre) and iron sulphate (in the proportion of forty gallons of a 15 per cent. solution to the acre) may be used with advantage. The chemical composition called lawn sand, sprinkled in dry weather on weeds, is said to burn them out, while at the same time acting as a fertiliser. Repairs having been completed, the whole green should be covered to a depth not exceeding the third of an inch or so, with a counterpane of sea sand, which will be absorbed by spring, feeding the turf and maintaining or replenishing its elasticity. In fact, every green is none the worse for this winter blanket. In February, should the grass of the repaired portions seem backward, a top-dressing of bone meal or soot may be applied. But no fertiliser should be employed that will force the grass to such an extent as to produce the thick velvety carpet that is apt to make the bowl drag in its progress towards the jack.

Kew Gardens are famous for their lawns.

There, according to Mr. W. J. Bean's *Royal Botanic Gardens, Kew*, weeds are uprooted by the spud. Vitriol dropped in the centre of weeds, or salt laid on them, is efficacious, provided the work be done with scrupulous care, but the process is very laborious and may cause disfigurement. For plantains, dandelions, and daisies he considers there is nothing better than a generous treatment of the grass, for it is where grass is thin and soil poor that weeds effect their firmest foothold. At Kew he finds that fine soil, rotted manure, or almost any kind of fine humus, thinly spread over the surface in February, is the simplest plan of renovating thin, poor grass. " Our experience at Kew with artificial manures as a top-dressing for lawns," he adds, " is not such as to lead us to recommend them. They stimulate the grass into great activity of growth for a short time, but produce no permanent benefit commensurate with the cost." The Kew practice applies to meadow turf, and Mr. Bean would himself admit that the sea turf of a Bowling green demands different treatment. The late Daniel Leslie, for instance, held it to be a great mistake to put soil either under or above turf on a green. " I have," he wrote, " made and re-laid a hundred and fifty greens without a spadeful of soil, and they are all living yet."

Worms—Nature's ventilators of the soil—are supposed to be the *bêtes noires* of green-layer and groundman alike. Readers, however, of Charles Darwin's classic monograph on *The Formation of Vegetable Mould through the Action of Worms* may entertain doubts on the subject. Though the turf on a Bowling green is not more than two inches in thickness, such a layer will accommodate the earthworm. Bowlers imagine that cinder and sand are inimical to worms, and probably this is the case within limits. Darwin, nevertheless, found grains of sand, small stones, rose thorns, and small splinters of glass in their gizzards, whilst he proved that the creatures also worked their way through old concrete and decayed mortar at Beaulieu Abbey and in Roman remains at Chedworth and Brading. They could burrow even through a layer of coarse cinders three and a half inches thick. Lime water will generally bring them to the surface, where the groundman can dispose of them, and he should also make a point of sweeping away the casts daily with his broom.

Leslie, on the other hand, considered worms a decided pest. " If a green is properly made by a practical man there will be no worms in it to begin with, if laid with sea turf, as worms will not live in turf overflowed by the tide." Leslie, on his part, was a trifle dogmatic,

WORMS AND THEIR CURE

for he overlooked the fact that worms do not always come upwards, but find their way to the turf from the surrounding banks and flower-beds; while, as for salt water, at all events a large class of marine worms revel in it, showing that the sea is not necessarily fatal to the worm kind. There are many ways, he says, of killing worms, but the trouble is to kill their eggs, for what will kill the *ova* will probably kill the grass, too. The most effective worm-killer he has found during a quarter of a century's experience is " corrosive sublimate (two ounces to a quart bottle) dissolved with a spoonful of alcohol and filled up with water. A wineglassful of this in two gallons of water, well mixed and put on with a watering-can, will bring them up in a hurry."

Climatically, Bowls may be played wherever suitable turf will establish itself, as has been abundantly demonstrated in Scotland. There are clubs in every shire in the kingdom, and Sir Alexander Rae, a bowler of many years' experience, who has known the town all his life, informs me that the greens in Wick are of undoubted excellence. Since matches are held annually, home and away, between Wick and Thurso, the latter on the Pentland Firth, it may be held as proved that the pastime is not barred anywhere within the length and breadth of Caledonia " stern and wild." Nay more,

Orcadians have made their game—even at midnight in the longest days—on greens at Kirkwall, built of native turf, which is, however, softer than that the Solway affords, and so plays rather on the dull side.

In Scotland the greens are mostly mown with the scythe, which, in the opinion of many, is the only instrument that should be used on a first-class green. But the majority of groundmen, in other respects well up to their work, cannot handle the scythe and perforce employ the lawn-mower, which is a capital substitute. To punch the green all over with a board set with big nails and fastened to a broomstick is a method of harrowing that gives good results in the way of ventilating the turf, the operation being sometimes accompanied with a " sowing " of sea sand.

Remarkable diversity of practice prevails in the weight of the roller. One Bowler who visited a large number of greens expressly to ascertain what the facts were was astonished to discover an extraordinary variety of weight, the rollers varying from two and a half cwts. to as much as ten and a half. The use of a half-ton roller is positively injurious to any green, as it cakes the surface, and binds and consolidates the turf, stifling growth and suffocating the grass. It is necessary to distinguish between the soft and tender meadow turf,

OF TRICKY GREENS 15

the least suitable covering for a green, and the hard, wiry, elastic turf which, laid *secundum artem*, is not a " preen the waur " after a season's wear and tear. Few greens require a roller of more than three cwts., and five cwts. should be regarded as the outside limit.

One common defect of most meadow-turf and a few sea-turf greens is " trickiness." It is mainly due to faulty construction and the foolish reluctance of clubs to " tamper with " a green after it has been laid. The fact is that every green without exception takes two or three years to settle down, and flaws may be looked for almost as a matter of course. The usual fault is a tendency to sink in parts, and should the turf not be raised and levelled at the spots, the green fails to run truly and becomes " tricky." Moreover, the foundation of the whole lawn sometimes falls in this or that direction, and a slope is developed, not visible to the naked eye, but quite obvious when a bowl travels over it. Ocular demonstration can always be had of the weak patches in a green by watching it during a prolonged downpour. The rain collects in all the depressions, however shallow and however numerous, and any Bowler will render his club a real service by then staking out the hollows, which the groundman shall afterwards correct.

Needless to say, a green must be perfectly

flat, looking just like a vast billiard-table, and respond with reasonable accuracy to the spirit-level.

A true green accounts for much. I have known protests lodged by English clubs against bowls of No. 3 bias—the smallest bias any self-respecting Bowler would use,—on the ground that they ran nearly straight on some greens. Instead, however, of pointing to insufficient bias, the objection indicated rather that the greens in question were so rough and poor that the grass held up the bowls and prevented them from taking their bias. The best bowls are turned for greens of presumed superlative quality, in normal weather true and keen, upon which players soon learn, in the words of a former Duke of Newcastle, to " do what they like with their own." Upon such greens a bowl of No. 3 bias would operate as to the manner born. Owing to their shape, the old-fashioned English bowls, rounder and smaller than those now in vogue and with enormous bias, roll over obstacles that would kill the bias of the heavier, more oblate, and more scientific bowls produced by the best present-day makers. On a perfect green these bowls of inordinate bias would monopolise nearly the whole of the lawn. The real remedy in the protests alluded to was, of course, to re-lay or improve the greens.

These considerations raise the old controversy of level greens *versus* crown greens, the latter type being almost exclusively confined to Lancashire, Yorkshire, some of the English Midland counties, and the Isle of Man. As its name implies, a crown green is a lawn, some forty yards square, or more, with a fall of from twelve to eighteen inches from the crown or centre all round to the ditch. It is usually played in singles with bowls of little bias and generally " all over the shop," that is, in any direction—up and down, diagonally, horizontally. Each player carries a wooden jack of similar bias to that of his bowls, which gives the first player a clear clue to the likely run of his bowls, thus rendering it incumbent upon him to watch the course of the jack from the moment he throws it until it come to rest. The utmost that can be urged in favour of the crown-green pastime is that it yields a sporting, though not a scientific game. Yet this admission must not be pushed too far. In a great pastime we have a right to look for qualities somewhat rarer and less fleeting than glorious uncertainty. One might perhaps get a sporting game on a billiard-table with the cloth split right across, but I fancy John Roberts, or H. W. Stevenson, or George Gray would soon sigh for a proper board.

What has always puzzled me about crown

greens is that they should ever have been constructed preferentially. Why a club laying down a new green should deliberately choose what has been ingenuously described as a " slightly uneven " lawn rather than a perfectly flat sheet of turf is one of those things that, in Lord Dundreary's words, " no fellow can understand." Presuming, therefore, that most men play Bowls for something more than mere sportiveness, such attributes as judgment, strategy, skill and science are demanded in a far higher degree on a level than on a crown green. Though tournaments for large sums of money do not affect the principle of the game, unhappily these inducements to play are growing more instead of less intimately associated with the crown-green pastime.

It is certain, too, that the level-green variety constitutes the historical game of Bowls, which one would expect *a priori*. In the infancy of every sport practice is necessarily crude and tentative. Rule of thumb prevails for many generations and codified laws only appear at a late stage. But this is not to say that in actual play men kept up a haphazard system year after year and decade after decade. An unwritten code develops inevitably. As in morals, the methods of play in this or that sport " rise on stepping-stones of their dead selves to higher things." The presumption,

THE GREENKEEPER

therefore, is reasonable that, all unchronicled though it be, the Bowlers of old went on improving their game in many directions. To suppose that they left the greens untouched, maintaining their pristine state of hillocks and hollows and other " unevennesses " is a hallucination.

It will be admitted that the post of groundman is no sinecure. Much of the superfine quality of Scottish greens is due to their admirable custodians. The Caledonian greenkeeper is a born genius, somewhat independent and critical, but a man of character and judgment, possessed of a proper sense of the dignity of labour. Many groundmen are deficient in initiative, not from ignorance so much as from backwardness. This shyness should be corrected, or the habit may grow chronic. Every groundman who is up to his work does not require to be told what to do. He only needs instructions about things concerning which he cannot be expected to have any knowledge. Those who make the most efficient greenkeepers are men in the employ of green-constructors, groundmen of cricket clubs, and gardeners, in the order given. When a club desires a man, the secretary should communicate with one of the leading contractors to ascertain whether he can recommend a suitable hand. It is important that the groundman should make himself thoroughly conversant with the laws of the game and, in his own interests, he ought to become an expert player, because he will occasionally be able to add to his wages by teaching a novice who is willing to pay for a few lessons.

When a club is fortunate enough to be served by a competent groundman, it should never part with him. Like the family doctor, he gets to know the constitution and life-history of his patient, and can treat it better than any committee can. The common difficulty is to keep the man going during the long close season. He should be placed on full wages from April 1st to October 31st, for the proper care of a fine full-sized green and the garden demands the exclusive attention of the keeper throughout the season. For one month before play begins he will be busy making ready, and for one month after play has ceased he will be occupied in repairing, altering, and cleaning up. " One green one man " is the only safe rule, so that clubs in possession of more than one green should bear this in mind. For the sake of discipline, however, it is then wiser to give to one of the men the position of Head Keeper. During the winter (when the groundman is at half-wage) the green will require attention from time to time, and, assuming that the keeper is an expert gardener, the members will be able to procure him a good deal of private custom. Sometimes, too, knowing that winter is his slack time, an industrious keeper qualifies himself in some trade which he may follow when " lyart leaves bestrow the yird," or the roaring game is in full blast. Moreover, clubs that possess commodious pavilions hold whist drives, smoking concerts, and other social entertainments during the dead vast and middle of the weary winter, and the groundman may officiate as general utility-man at all such functions.

Bowlers are notoriously sociable and hospitable, but they must not tempt the greenkeeper. The Irishman welcomed temptation, for that it gave him an opportunity to fall; but this should be denied to the groundman. They can have no objection to his smoking—it seems to fit in with his occupation,—but they should discourage tippling and tipping. It is, of course, legitimate to pay for services specially rendered (such as dressing the bowls with ronuk), but habitual tipping must be discountenanced. Human nature is human nature and, consciously or not, a groundman tipped is apt to think that he is expected to render a *quid pro quo*.

Every club owning a green worthy of the name and the fame appoints a ranger or a green rota, armed with full powers for its maintenance and protection. They are administrators of the green and to them in this capacity the groundman will look for instructions. They will give him orders about matches (how many rinks will be wanted, and so forth) and it is their duty to see that the lawn is never played on when, in their judgment, the state of the weather renders it inadvisable to do so. When the committee is asked for the loan of a rink or two, or possibly for the whole green (as neutral ground for the playing of an important match or handicap), the ranger or the rota will carry out all necessary arrangements through the groundman. (In this particular it should be said, in parenthesis, that clubs in possession of perfect greens should not be chary of granting such requests, provided the occasion really justifies them. It invariably helps the game to show visiting clubs and Bowlers a green that is probably, and perhaps far, better than their own. Committees, therefore, under adequate safeguards, ought never to miss a chance of " spreading the light.") The rota will make the wearing of rubber-soled shoes imperative on the part of all players. The Australian practice of using a mat big enough to take the stride of the Bowler in the act of delivering his bowl has everything in its favour, and rangers should insist upon the use of large footers, to save the green. The ranger or rota will not

THE GOLDEN RULE

employ their powers arbitrarily or unwarrantably, although they must cultivate the strength of will to forbid play, even to themselves, when there is the smallest likelihood of the lawn suffering damage if played upon. All Bowlers recognise the ethical value of their game and learn patience and self-denial with becoming resignation. The Golden Rule is—Always give the green the benefit of the doubt.

CHAPTER II

THE FLOWING BOWL

"Bools and the Man"—The Stone Age—The Age of Wood—Excelite—What is a Bowl?—What is Bias?—Loading with Lead—Messrs. Barclay and Perkins's Tudor Bowls—*Lignum vitæ*—The Making of a Bowl—The Turner's Art—The "Eyes," or Ivories—The Testing-Room—Varnished—Veining of the Wood—Weight of the Bowls—Bowls in Ronuk—Too Narrow Bias—The English B.A. and Bias—What *is* a Standard Bowl's Bias?—The Proper Bias—Under-sized Bowls.

OUR Epic having now become, in *quasi*-Carlylean phraseology, *Bools and the Man*, let us consider the bowl, or tool with which the game is played. Passing from the Stone Age with the remarks elsewhere offered thereanent (p. 4), we proceed to the Age of Wood, still in lusty vigour, noting as we go, however, that there has set in a Period of Excelite, a composition bowl, highly spoken of by many players and described as of equal density throughout, well balanced, and proof against cracking and warping.

According to the *New English Dictionary*, a bowl is "a body of hard wood, originally spherical, but now made slightly oblate on one side and prolate on the other, so as to run with a bias." If it ever existed, the vogue of spherical bowls cannot have lasted long, for, as we know from Shakspere and other early writers, bias was already the distinctive feature in a bowl, which was frequently referred to as the "biassed bowl." The same authority defines bias as "a term at Bowls, applied alike to the construction or form of the bowl imparting an oblique motion, the oblique line in which it runs, and the kind of impetus given to cause it to run obliquely." John Norris, in his *Treatise Concerning Christian Prudence*, correctly observes that "the bowl will run, not as the Hand directs, but as the Bias leads"; and Alexander Pope, in *The Dunciad*, showed that his visits to the green had not been paid in vain :—

> O thou, of bus'ness the directing soul!
> To this our head like byass to the bowl,
> Which, as more pond'rous, made its aim more true,
> Obliquely waddling to the mark in view.

Horace Smith, one of the authors of *Rejected Addresses*, in his *Tin Trumpet*, neatly remarks, " It is not every rogue that, like a bowl, can gain his object the better by deviating from the straight line."

There were two ways of obtaining bias. One of these was the clumsy device of fastening lead to one side of the bowl. Did we not know of its use from other sources, Dr. Johnson leaves us in little doubt on the subject, for, bias is, says he, " the weight lodged on one side of the bowl, which turns it from the straight line." On the other hand, Robert Recorde, the mathematician's, allusion, in the *Castle of Knowledge*, would apply indifferently to loading with lead or turning in the lathe, the alternative way by which bias was given to a bowl and now the only way. " A little altering of the one side," he remarks, " maketh the bowl to run biasse waies."

Probably the lathe was used from the first for better-class bowls. By the courtesy of Messrs. Barclay and Perkins, the famous brewers, I was privileged to examine nine bowls that were unearthed in the course of excavations for an extension of their immense premises in the ancient borough of Southwark. They are made of yew or box, and bear no trace of lead. On the contrary, the bias-bulge is very pronounced and was no doubt effected by the lathe. They are of the size of the archaic English bowl I have elsewhere (p. 144) alluded to. All things considered, they are in excellent preservation. They have, of course, lost their outward beauty—the varnish has gone; the " eyes " have vanished, though the sockets remain; and the wood has cast a few flakes. Whether they are of Tudor age,

LIGNUM VITÆ

as has been alleged, is matter of conjecture. But it was not without emotion that a Bowler of the 20th century sat in Dr. Johnson's easy-chair and handled bowls that might have swept a Southwark green what time Shakspere was acting hard by at The Globe.

In these days, when perfect greens have raised the game to a fine art, only the best bowls will allow of scientific play, and manufacturers, on their mettle, are producing " woods " of vastly improved craftsmanship. Superior bowls are made of the finest *lignum vitæ*, a dense, heavy wood, often beautifully veined, furnished by *Guaiacum officinale*, a tree indigenous to San Domingo and other islands in the West Indies. In maturity it attains to a height of from thirty to fifty feet and its trunk measures from thirty to forty-two inches in circumference. Polished sections of the timber as well as specimens of the huge resinous tears which the tree sheds are exhibited in the museum of the Royal Botanic Gardens at Kew, where also—in one of the houses devoted to the Economical Plants—may be seen striplings in actual growth. The heartwood is dark greenish brown in colour, and the sapwood (the wood next the bark) yellow. The timber is usually supplied to Bowl-makers in billets or logs about six feet long and ten inches in diameter.

By the permission of Messrs. F. H. Ayres, Limited, of Aldersgate Street, London, I was enabled to see the whole process of making a bowl from start to finish. Their factory is equipped with the latest tools, some of their own inventing, and employs a large number of skilled artisans. The cellars are stacked with many varieties of wood and from a log of *lignum vitæ* two portions, about six inches long, were sawn off for my benefit. These were then deprived of their sapwood by the swiftly-revolving saw and converted into polygons. In this condition they are ready for the lathe and are speedily changed by the turner, first into barrel-shaped objects and afterwards into oblate spheroids, or bowls in their roughest form.

At this stage, in the ordinary course, they would be put away in a cool, airy, well-ventilated apartment for a twelvemonth in order that the wood should become perfectly seasoned and defects, if any, disclose themselves. In the present instance, however, this interval was dispensed with for my advantage, and the turner proceeded to impart bias. The details of the process by which this is accomplished are a trade secret, but the machine acts with exquisite accuracy—as is, indeed, essential—and provides whatever bias—3, 4, or more—may be desired. The

THE MAKING OF A BOWL

greater the bulge or convexity the greater is the bias on a bowl. If you cannot detect the biassed side of a bowl of narrow bias, hold it against the sky and you will then discover it, but on a standard bowl the bias ought to be patent to the eye. An entirely spherical bowl, it is obvious, could not circumvent any obstacle or describe a curvilinear path. No. 3 is the smallest bias allowed by law : hence on an inferior green, the Bowler, though using the same bowl, would have to allow for a narrower draw.

When the biassed side of the bowl answers to the template, or testing gauge, with the utmost nicety, the ornamentation or " beading " is furnished by the appropriate instruments, and then the holes are gouged for the " eyes " or ivories—the larger hole on one side for the ivory that is to bear the initials or name of the bowler, the smaller on the other side for the ivory that is to carry the number (1, 2, 3, 4) of the bowl.

Of course the bowl has not been treated as a whole at any stage in its making ; first one half is modelled and then the other. The bowl is, however, not quite finished yet. Though the eye may not notice it, a delicate touch will detect a certain roughness of surface. This is remedied by the application of sand-paper as well as some of the shavings of this very bowl, which, under this treatment, soon becomes as smooth as a baby's cheek. The sandpaper removes the roughness, the shavings remove any the most infinitesimal traces of grit that the sandpaper may have left.

Next, the bowl is taken to the large testing-room, the floor of which has been specially constructed to a dead level, and the bias of the bowl in movement is now rigidly tested. The track of a bowl of normal bias is marked on the floor and the new bowl must take this bias at least, on the way to the jack, before it is exposed to the finishing touches. The floor represents the green on a smaller scale and the measurements bear in every respect an exact proportion to those of an actual rink of the lawn.

Having passed this test—and not till then—a varnish, concocted according to a special recipe, is next applied which will both develop and enhance the natural beauty of the wood. Manufacturers have shown an unfortunate tendency to reduce the finished bowls to a common standard of blackness which leads most people to suppose them made of ebony. When the markings of *lignum vitæ* are remarkably fine—and this is by no means rare in bowls of the highest class—it is a pity to shroud them under a cloak of darkness.

From the time this pair of bowls was sawn

from the log until they were ready for the testing-room the process lasted a solid hour, throughout which period the turner relaxed neither vigilance nor interest. The rough blocks sawn from the log weighed 7 lbs. a piece and when finished, but without the ivory eyes (which would not materially affect their weight), turned the scale at 3 lbs. 6 oz. each. In fact in the scales the one bowl exactly balanced the other, a result that eloquently testified to the turner's skill and art.

It is impossible to say how long a bowl will continue fit for match play. I won a pair of Taylor's make in 1890 and they are still in constant use. In fact good bowls, properly cared for, will last for a very long time. At the close of the season they should be thickly smeared with ronuk and allowed to lie in this throughout the winter. The coating may be renewed, if need be. Then on the eve of the opening day the ronuk will be rubbed off—more power to your elbow!—and you will carry to the green two pairs of brilliantly-polished bowls ready for action.

Abuses of bias too frequently crop up. Bowlers in possession of bowls stamped as of No. 3 bias have been accused of getting them turned down to No. 2 or less. It is unnecessary to stigmatise such a practice. The marvel is that in a community of sportsmen it should ever have been tolerated, and it is incredible that any manufacturer of repute should aid and abet it. However, the English Bowling Association having had its attention drawn to this scandal, appointed in 1909–10 a sub-committee to investigate the methods of bias-testing employed by the leading Bowl-makers. There was reason to fear that, at the outset, a mistake in tactics might endanger the inquiry, but happily the manufacturers so far from resenting inspection, as an interference with possibly secret trade processes, welcomed it and, in the great majority of cases, facilitated the labours of the sub-committee. What the English B.A. aimed at was to prevent bowls of smaller bias than that, at least, of the standard from being placed on the market, Bowlers pleasing themselves about a wider bias, for with that the Association has no concern. In consequence of the makers' co-operation (all the more valuable that it was so largely spontaneous), it was confidently anticipated that the continued use of bowls of narrower bias than the normal would cease.

Considerable difficulty exists as to what the bias of a standard bowl really is, but the allegation that the Scottish B.A. has passed bowls drawing four and four-and-a-half feet to a thirty-yard jack on a normal green in fine

SMALL BOWLS

weather can have no foundation in fact. It is, however, essential that the law should explicitly state what is the bias of a standard No. 3. This should stipulate in effect that a bowl of approved bias shall draw not fewer than six feet to a thirty-yard jack on a dry green of average Scottish quality.

Under-sized bowls — of no use to any but the owners—are met with only on the poorer English greens, on which the pastime is still played according to Rule of Thumb. " Tradition," says Whittier, " wears a snowy beard " and custom dies hard. Such bowls will probably disappear with the users of them. They are barred for three good and sufficient reasons —first, they are too small; second, they are too light; third, they have not enough bias. Doubtless, heretical timber may be seen on many greens, despite the utmost vigilance of the powers that be. Small bowls, however, never appear on Scottish greens and their use elsewhere will cure itself when lawns generally are " tuned up to concert pitch," and the manifold subtleties of the game are universally appreciated.

CHAPTER III

THE RUDIMENTS

Buying Bowls—Swear Words—Throwing the Jack—Winning the Toss—Defects of the Scots Law—The English Practice — That an Unstraightened Jack is Playable — Various Names for the Jack — Bias in Action — Forehand and Backhand Play — Visualise the Track of your Bowl!—Wrong Bias—Cultivate Play on Both Hands—Style and Attitude—Different Attitudes considered — Delivering the Bowl — Throwing and Dumping—The Right Mode of Delivery—How to Hold the Bowl—Playing on a Soft Green—" Be up " and " Take green "!

In theory the game of Bowls is simplicity itself: the principle of play is so readily grasped and the means to an end are apparently so straightforward. What is easier to say and comprehend than that all a Bowler has to do, is to roll his bowls as close to the jack as he can, and that the player who has one or more bowls nearer than the nearest of his opponent's adds one or more shots to his score? It is easy, so *very* easy! Yet in its severely simple character lie the game's fascination and its snare. Strategy must be subtle in a sport in which the adversaries are

THE RIGHT BOWLS

well matched and the tools are few and alike. But there is no royal road to excellence and he who would excel must begin at the beginning.

Buying the Bowls

What the novice has to do first, then, is to play with his own bowls. He should purchase two pairs of bowls and make a point of getting to know their behaviour in all kinds of weather on various kinds of green, for almost every pair of bowls has its own characteristics. The laws prescribe the maximum of a bowl's size (16½ inches in circumference) and weight (3½ pounds) and stipulate that its bias shall not be less than that of a standard bowl.

Some men have short dumpy hands and find it difficult to manipulate a very full size. Therefore, before effecting his purchase, the Bowler should handle the bowls and procure those he can hold quite comfortably. This is important, for unless he feels perfectly at ease with his weapons, he will not play as good a game as he otherwise might; for his hands will not grow larger and the full-sized bowl will not grow smaller. And it will be useless to fall back upon the stale excuse of the poor workman and blame his tools, if he commit the initial error of buying the wrong ones. Similar considerations apply to weight, with this proviso that it is a serious mistake to use light bowls. Try the balance of the bowl in the hand; weigh it, as it were; and if you feel that it suits your hand and goes well with the swing of the arm, that will be the weight for you. Other things being equal, however, there is every reason why the Bowler should acquire bowls of the maximum size and weight. As to bias, most players use No. 3, but I like to work with two bowls of this, and two of somewhat bigger bias.

On some English greens only one pair of bowls is used, but on all greens of capital quality on which the Scottish code is accepted, four bowls are used in singles and two and four a-side friendlies, but only two bowls in matches. In Scotland, in what is termed " rink " play—four-a-side games—each player uses two bowls; only in single-handed or pairs games are four bowls used. Having obtained bowls to his liking, the player should induce a friend to coach him in the art of drawing to the jack. At first he should play with men who are decidedly his superiors and study their play. Much in that way is to be learnt,—as well what to eschew as what to emulate.

Swear Words

Leigh Hunt says, in his *Autobiography*, that, while disclaiming any special merit for the fact, swearing was, somehow or other, never a habit in his family. When he was a boy, being anxious to know what it was like, he once snatched a fearful joy in the utterance of the words, " Damn it." For long afterwards he felt quite miserable and every time he was praised and patted on the head, he could not help thinking, " Ah ! they little suspect that I am the boy who said ' Damn it.' "

Speaking for myself, I have seldom found Bowls provocative. During a captaincy of twenty-five years, complaint was only once made to me by one of my skips of the language used by his opponent. The culprit, it appeared, was a village blacksmith and probably garnished his talk without meaning much harm.

Why are some games more stimulative to " swear words " than others ? I state it simply as my experience and not at all as a matter of boasting, that unparliamentary language is not customary on Bowling greens. Now, in golf usage is quite different, not excluding even the cloth. There is the well-known story of the man who asked a caddie on St. Andrews links whether he had seen Principal Tulloch on the course. " Ou, ay ! " answered the caddie, " ye'll find him oot by, teein' his ba' an' damnin' awfu'!" When the Rev. John McNeill, the well-known missioner, was learning gowff, his partner on one occasion uttered a hearty "Damn." Thereupon the minister laid his hand on his rival's shoulder and said, "My friend, that stroke wasn't worth a damn." Whether as rebuke or criticism, or both, that subtle retort was perfect.

So far as the green is concerned, however, Bowlers will probably agree with Bob Acres that "damns have had their day." Yet were this circumstance to be used in prejudice of the game, it might be necessary to consider the situation from the point of view of wee Leigh Hunt.

Throwing the Jack

At the beginning of a game, the jack is tossed for by the leaders. If you win the toss, throw the jack. This is a purely conventional use of the word, for the jack is really rolled along the green. In a single-handed game, it would be foolish to allow your adversary the privilege of throwing the jack you had won, and in a rink-set it is only the conceited skip who bids his leader let his opponent have the jack. Such a skip "fancies" himself as a player of the last bowl, and he secures this right by giving up the jack, although his leader has won the toss. It is a

PLACING THE MAT

distinct advantage for a leader to play to a clear jack, and *he* should have consideration and not the skip. Nevertheless, as a matter of discipline, should the skip insist upon his vanity being humoured, the leader has no alternative but to hand over the jack to his rival. But, as a rule, if you win the jack you will be allowed to throw it.

It is one of the courtesies of the game for the leader who does not throw the jack to place the mat from which the jack is thrown and the bowls are delivered. This custom is to be respected at the beginning of every end. The mat should be placed quite straight and in the centre of the rink in a line with the plate which bears the number of the rink and indicates the exact middle of the space. At the start the mat will be laid down about three feet from the ditch, but in all later heads it must either be placed where the jack lay when the previous end was finished, provided it be centred in a horizontal line with that spot, or placed at any place backwards between that point and the ditch; it must never be laid in front of the spot where the jack lay.

Decidedly the slovenliest habit the Bowler can be guilty of is an indolent way of throwing the jack. This fault exists on all greens, but I am not sure that the greatest sinners are not to be found in Scottish clubs. The jack *must* be thrown at least twenty-five yards from the mat (a minimum jack) and not farther than two yards from the ditch (a maximum jack). No objection can be taken to these limits which, in the case of a full-sized green, forty-two yards square, afford a margin of twelve to fourteen yards for jacks of varying length, though it is an open question whether twenty-three yards would not prove a more useful minimum. The monotony of bowling to jacks of uniform length, whether long or short, will scarcely be disputed. Every Bowler should accustom himself to throwing jacks of all lengths—short, medium, and long,—for the art is useful in singles and matches alike; and he should always try to throw the jack straight up the rink, making it follow an imaginary line bisecting the space into two equal portions.

With singular want of thought, the Scottish lawgivers stipulated that when the jack is thrown " less than two yards from the ditch it should be *moved out* to that distance." Instead of requiring it, in that event, to be thrown afresh by the other side, the law positively rewards the slovenly thrower by giving him a maximum jack to bowl to. And I venture to assert that a full-length jack is probably the very jack a player of that sort likes best. When, therefore, he has obtained

STRAIGHTENING THE JACK 41

possession of the jack, he has only to throw it nearly into the ditch and he will always get a full-length jack,—until he happens to lose an end.

But this is not the only foul throw for which the slovenly player may plead legislative countenance, for in another section of the law it is declared that if the jack " run to one side it *shall be moved* straight across and placed in the line of the pins numbering the rinks." This moving of the jack by some one not the thrower is a direct incentive to slovenliness. In order to appreciate the laxity of the Scots law, however, it will be helpful to consider the custom that once prevailed—and is not yet extinct—amongst clubs in London and the South of England. They recognised what the Scottish legislators missed, namely, that the provisions as to a maximum jack supplied a clue to the treatment of a jack which, when it had ceased running, was wide of the median line. If a full-length jack must be six feet from the ditch, why not adapt that requirement to the side boundaries also? Accordingly this became almost the universal custom in the South and Midlands. So regarded, a jack was a legal jack which when it came to rest was twenty-five yards from the mat and at least six feet from all boundaries, that is, from the ditch and each of the side threads or strings. There was absolute precision in such practice The player was obliged to throw a jack that complied with clearly defined conditions, and the moving (or kicking) of the jack into the central line was therefore not only unnecessary but strictly forbidden, and, in point of fact, unknown. On greens where this custom obtained, it did not pay to be slovenly, because the leader tried to throw the jack which he or his side preferred.

That a jack which is off the straight may yet be readily played to can be demonstrated both by English practice and, *mirabile dictu,* Scottish rules. In the accompanying diagram the position before bowling, according to these laws, is represented by the vertical median line MJ, where M is the mat and J the jack. No matter how far from the middle line the jack had rolled (within the limits of the rink), it is always moved, in the Scottish custom, to the central line. Suppose it had been thrown to the spot K, which is more than six feet from the end and side boundaries, it would not, in the old English practice, be moved out to the middle line, but be played to where it lies. The course of the bowl on the forehand, MFK, shows that this is easily possible without breach of any law, and so followers of the ancient English game suffer the jack to remain where it has been thrown. How-

THE OLD ENGLISH JACK

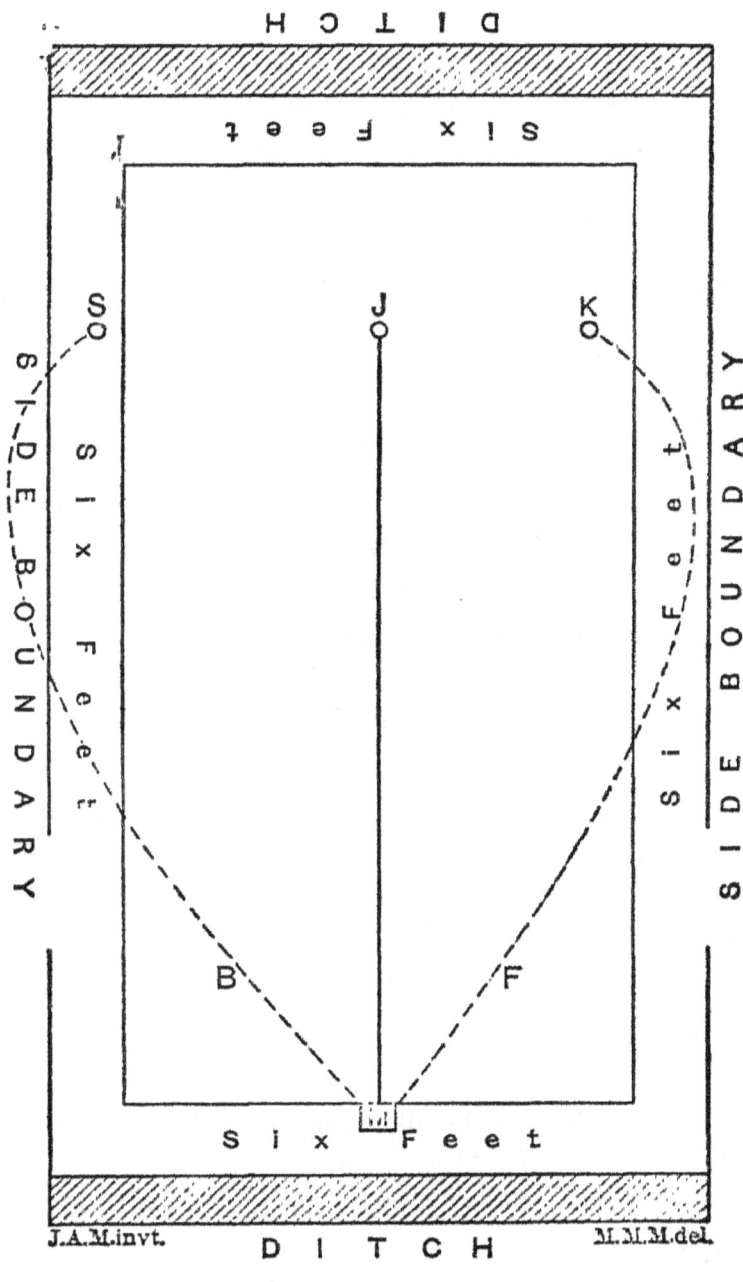

The Unstraightened Jack.

ever, should it come to rest within the six-feet limit, they move it as far out as that distance, but no farther. Now, consider a position that frequently arises on greens where the Scots laws are in vogue. Imagine that the third man's first bowl has " cut " the jack to S. Though now only four feet from the side boundary, it is still alive, *and must be played to.* The track MBS shows how it may be reached even on the backhand, for though the bowl has travelled outside of the side boundary altogether, this is legitimate as long as it returns within the playing space before it has ceased to run : should it remain outside, it becomes a dead bowl, and must be removed to the end bank.

In consequence of the vicious system that has grown up under the ægis of the Scots law, many Bowlers throw the jack " anyhow," knowing that it will be centred. I have seen it flung with a jerk from the level of the hip as if it were a missile, or chucked diagonally into an adjoining rink. On many greens, so thoroughly has sheer laziness become ingrained, two jacks are requisitioned, one for each end of the playing space. This indolent custom has the further drawback that it tends to foster playing to jacks of uniform length, and this of full size.

Yet there is a virtue even in the throwing

of a jack. It is not thrown for the fun of the thing, but should be delivered with as much care as the bowl. The object of throwing it is threefold. In the first place, it conveys to the player some hint of strength and length; secondly, he (or his side) may have a preference for a jack of given length, and he will naturally endeavour to throw it accordingly; and thirdly, he will soon discover, if he keep his weather-eye open, that his opponent also has a preference, and will therefore, as a wise man, make it his business to throw a baulking jack. It must surely be plain that these advantages are neutralised by the sloven. It is equally clear that no Bowler will ever become a proficient leader who ignores them, and may even jeopardise his chance of a place in a match team. Therefore the surest method of training leaders is strictly to discourage the random throwing of the jack in the ordinary daily play. In Bowls it is as easy to acquire good style as bad, and it ought to be a mere truism to insist that there is a right way of throwing the jack.

"Jack," in the Bowler's sense, is at least as old as Shakspere (p. 18). It was also formerly called the "block," the "mark," and the "mistress," which last designation may perhaps explain the name of "kitty," as generic for "woman," by which it is known in some quarters. None of the lexicographers recognises " kitty " as a synonym for " jack," and one would rather expect any word-play of this sort to have yielded the form " jill." There is a Scots diminutive " kitty " meaning " a small bowl " (basin), and mayhap some wiseacre, " rushing in where angels fear to tread," confounded the bowls and unblushingly gave us " kitty " as an alternative to " jack." But I think that " kitty " as generic for " woman," deriving through " mistress," is the most probable explanation.

Bias in Action

To the beginner bias necessarily presents some difficulty. Bias, he has learned, is on the bowl, not " on the green," as is said of the crown-green game. At first he may think to attain the jack by delivering his bowl straightforward upon it. Let him do so by way of experiment and instruction, and he will soon see the bowl curving away to the right or left in obedience to the bias, and anywhere rather than towards the jack. Similarly, were his bowls spherical, without bias at all, he would only need mentally to measure the length of the jack and gauge the strength of the green—and abandon Bowls for ever, as a puerile pastime. For the want of bias transforms the ruling principle of the game into something purely mechanical at the best.

Now, bias in action introduces a cardinal feature—the two methods of play which every Bowler must cultivate, namely, the forehand and backhand (Fig. 1). These he must assiduously study, knowing no rest on the green until he has completely mastered both. Forehand play consists in bowling on the right hand from the mat to the jack, and backhand in bowling on the left. (All Bowlers naturally left-handed will simply reverse these actions—*their* forehand would be on the left from mat to jack, their backhand on the right.) What the Bowler virtually does is to picture in his mind's eye a straight line between the mat and the jack, and then deliver the bowl a few feet on the right of such a line for forehand play, or a few feet on the left for backhand. Every Bowler should acquire the capacity of *visualising the track of the bowl he is about to deliver* to suit the precise position of things at the moment. That is why Bowlers like a well-lighted green.

Just how many feet the bowl will draw depends upon several things, of which the player must take cognisance. The chief considerations are (*a*) the state of the green, (*b*) the length of the jack, and (*c*) the amount of bias his bowls carry. After wet weather the

48 THE RUDIMENTS

green will be heavy and draw less bias; in hot weather it will pull the normal bias (Fig. 1); and after a long-continued spell of heat, it

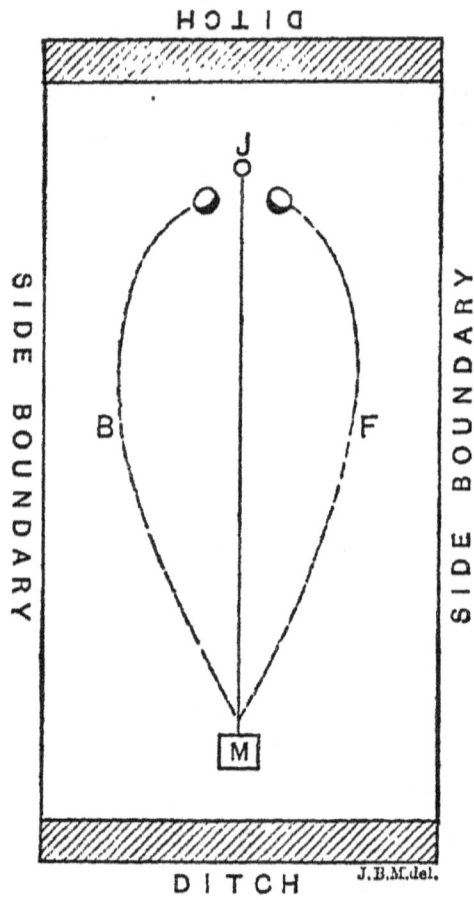

FIG. 1.—BIAS ACTING NORMALLY.
MFJ, Fore; MBJ, Back hand.

will play so fast that it will draw the heaviest bias his bowls can take.

Before delivering it the player ought to

THE RULE AS TO BIAS 49

glance at the bowl to see that he is playing with and not against the bias, whether on the fore or the back hand. The rule is ex-

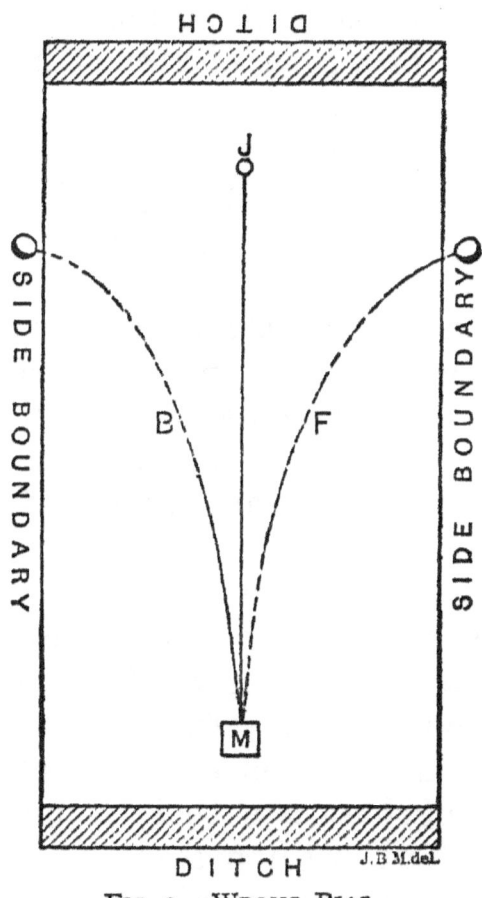

Fig. 2.—Wrong Bias.

Bowl on Fore hand, F, has been delivered with Back hand bias.
„ Back „ B, „ „ „ Fore „ „

tremely simple—whether he play fore hand or whether he play back, he must always keep the biassed half of the bowl innermost.

If he neglect this precaution, he may afford the spectators great amusement without benefiting his side in the least (Fig. 2). Veterans occasionally make this mistake, and I have seen a case of wrong bias even in an international game.

Moreover, the novice must be careful not to force the bias in any way. The bias will act of itself at the proper moment. Whenever I have noticed a Bowler give the bowl a sort of twist in the article of delivery, I have invariably found on inquiry that, before taking up Bowls, the player had been a bowler in a cricket club. I was always assured either that he was unconscious of the action or did it from force of habit. In any case it is a defect, and must be corrected.

There is a natural preference for forehand play, because in bowling to the right the arm swings without effort with the body, while in backhand play the arm has to cross the body with a swing in which there is more or less conscious effort, with perhaps an unacknowledged sense of awkwardness, in order to deliver the bowl to the left. Yet it is so essential to be able to play either hand freely, that I do not exaggerate the importance of the art when I impress on every beginner the three things necessary to make a Bowler—first, forehand and backhand play; second,

THE ONE THING NEEDFUL 51

forehand and backhand play; third, forehand and backhand play. Nevertheless, because forehand play is, so to speak, a natural movement, responding readily to the poise and swing of the human frame, many Bowlers obstinately acquire it, and it alone. In answer to repeated remonstrances, they have declared their inability to play backhand, as if it were something that demanded exceptional study, like the binomial theorem or the Russian language, for which they had neither time nor inclination. But it must be said plainly once for all that every Bowler who does not cultivate backhand as well as forehand play knows only half of the art and science of the game and misses more than half of its charm. What would this uninstructed Bowler think of a batsman who could only hit to " leg " and " on," and refused to learn cutting and " off " play ?

Style and Attitude

Another gift the beginner should acquire is a graceful, easy delivery. Not that a becoming style will of itself make a Bowler—on the contrary, many crack players have desperately ugly styles,—but a man plays none the worse for feeling free, comfortable, and unconstrained. It is also a boon to the spectators.

There was nothing more attractive to watch than the supreme ease with which Frank Shatford, of Kettering, drew to the jack in his contest with M. Turner, of Carlisle, on the fine green of the Upper Clapton Club on July 25th, 1910; and there was constant pleasure in following the perfect grace of John Forman, of Edinburgh; or the lissom elegance of J. R. Chapman, of Sunderland, and Sam Windrim, of Belfast; or the supple deliveries of Harry Childs, of Reading; or the deadly *insouciance* of J. S. Emmerson, of Carlisle Edenside B.C.; or the art-concealing-art liveliness of James Gillespie Carruthers.

Whether a great player or only an indifferent one, every Bowler adopts his own attitude at the mat : it is, in fact, the thing that gives him individuality. It would, therefore, be absurd to affirm positively that one position was more helpful than another. Speaking generally, however, one of five positions is favoured—the upright, the stoop, the stride, the kneeling, and the " hunkerswise." In the first, the bowler stands bolt upright, visualises the track he wishes his bowl to pursue (especially studying—as all Bowlers must, no matter what their attitude—whatever his skip may have asked him to do), and then, having laid his plan, takes one step forwards, drops easily and delivers his bowl with a free and yet

ATTITUDE AT THE MAT

deliberate sweep of the arm, the swing being carried through and completed after the bowl has left his hand. In the second, the Bowler stands on the mat, his body bent in a stooping posture and his bowl almost touching the green. When he has taken in the situation, he delivers the bowl with scarcely any action. Though it may look a stiff and constrained attitude, it is largely affected. The stride, which is commonly adopted by Bowlers who stand six feet in their socks, is a modification of the stoop. With one foot on the mat, the player takes an enormous stride forwards with the other and holds the bowl almost on the turf. Having surveyed his land, he then launches the wood. In the fourth, the Bowler, resting his hand on his left knee, appears to kneel on the mat with his right leg, and so delivers the bowl. This attitude ensures much steadiness of aim. In the fifth, the player bends his left leg and appears to sit on the heels of his right, which is drawn up beneath him, but does not fall into the kneeling position; then he delivers the bowl either without change of position, or, rising slightly, takes a short step forwards and launches the bowl. Attitude, as I have hinted, is a matter of taste, but as a beginner must adopt some attitude, and I use the upright myself, I need not hesitate to recommend him to cultivate it. The fifth, or "hunkers" fashion, has always struck me as ungainly and needlessly cramping the Bowler, and the learner may at least dispense with *it*.

Delivering the Bowl

If the golfer who hacks and hews, not the putting green but the outfield, is looked upon as a pariah by his fellows, it is by comparison impossible to designate the Bowler whose clumsy carelessness "skins" the Bowling green, which is as much superior to the putting green as the latter is to the outfield. Yet the Bowler far more easily than the golfer can avoid any damage to the turf. Injury to the green is almost entirely caused by faulty delivery of the bowl. Beginners err through ignorance, and older players through culpable laziness and indifference. The former throw, the latter dump the bowl, and just as the perpetual drip-drip of water will hollow out the hardest stone, a succession of such deliveries continued over even a short space of time will infallibly strip the grass and make bare patches and indentations big enough to modify the exact running of the "woods." The whole art of right delivery consists in getting well down to the surface of the green and, in the very act of launching the bowl,

THROWING AND DUMPING

taking care that *the hand and turf make one plane.* Thus delivered, the bowl should glide from the hand, like a ship's hull from the builder's slip. There should not be the shadow of a suspicion of a throw. One may always tell when a bowl has been imperfectly delivered, though perhaps not actually thrown. When it begins its career with a wobbling action and " shows its eyes," this is a certain sign that the bowler has been too hasty. It may be said without exaggeration that every defect in the delivery affects to some extent the true course of the bowl. Occasionally the bowl may right itself, but even then it does not perform its work so effectively as it would had it been despatched on its way without a hitch.

Therefore, the beginner must learn from the very first to roll and not pitch the bowl. In the case of old players the defect is usually past remedy, for they will not take the necessary trouble to bend low enough to enable the hand to form a true plane with the turf. Their conduct is really reprehensible, for probably they began and continued for years to deliver their bowls well and truly. It is when they put on flesh and fancy their knees are stiff that so many of them will not stoop, but send the bowl to the green with a dump. From close observation of several of these hardened sinners, I am satisfied they need never acquire the habit in the first place, and, in the second, may readily cure it if it grow upon them unconsciously. These dumpers do so much harm to the lawn that one must frankly confess their active participation in the game has ceased to be desirable.

From what has been said about the damage done by throwing the bowl, Bowls should be forbidden on a soft green, when the turf has become sodden and relaxed by heavy rain and is in such a tender state that it responds very quickly to usage that might not affect a dry green. Whenever one can trace the track of bowls, like the wake of a steamer, it is certain play has been going on when the ground was too damp and when the ranger or rota should have closed the green.

In delivering the bowl, it should be held a *leetle* loosely in the palm of the hand and " steadied " in its place by the thumb and forefinger. One sometimes hears of the " Bowler's grip." The expression is unhappy, since it implies that the bowl should be held tightly. There is, however, one shot in which it is really necessary to hold the bowl very firmly, and that is the drive. In the case of all other deliveries ease of handling the bowl rather than any method of holding it with a grip is essential, if the bowl is to run from the hand with a free and graceful course towards

ADVICE TO BEGINNERS

the jack. And, by the by, though the player should not be in a hurry to deliver his bowl, he must at the same time beware of mentally studying his intended course too long: in such event he is in danger of "oversighting" himself, and his bowl will probably run either too narrow and short, or too wide and strong.

"Be Up"

"Never up, never in" is the standing caution to the tyro in golf when he has reached the putting green. Similarly, "Be up" is one of the earliest pieces of advice to be tendered to the young Bowler. For weak play to the jack is the besetting sin of every beginner, almost without exception. Happily this failing, though serious, lends itself to easy remedy. It arises almost inevitably from ignorance of the precise amount of force required to send the bowl from the mat towards the other end of the green. Nevertheless, the defect must be cured without delay, for it is one of the worst faults a Bowler can commit, since the blocking of the draw to the jack, either on the fore or back hand, not only spoils his own game but that of his fellows, while in a match it is heart-breaking to the skip. For though short play is the brand of the novice, I have seen it on the part of leaders even in international matches, when, of course, it is due to temporary failure of nerve. The beginner will be well advised to play strongly to the jack, for if his bowl should run beyond the tee, at all events it can do no harm there, being out of everybody's road, and may even become useful; and, moreover, in actual experience it is found easier to moderate the force of strong play than to work up from feebleness to the proper length. A bowl is better in the ditch than too short, for a short bowl catches the eye of the later Bowlers until the end is played out, besides being an obstacle of no value whatever to the player's side. Full length and full bias are priceless in Bowling. One must therefore inculcate these maxims repeatedly on every beginner—" Be up " and " Take green " !

CHAPTER IV

THE RINK GAME

The word "Rink"—The Quartet of Players—He who Must be Obeyed—Discipline and Combination—THE LEADER—THE SECOND PLAYER—Card of the Match—THE THIRD MAN—THE SKIP—Knowledge of Human Nature—The Unsuitable Man—"What do you see?"—Discreet Praise of his Men—The Noisy Skip—The Policy of Firing—Carrying the Jack—The Question of Guarding—Watch the Measure — Win Well and Lose Well—"Touchers"—Spat upon *Honoris Causa*—"Ditchers"—The "Live Jack"—English Practice Preferable—The Captain.

IT is unfortunate that the word "rink" is used in a twofold sense in Bowls. Sometimes it is employed to describe the playing space, and sometimes it implies the quartet of men who play upon it. Usually the context renders the meaning clear, yet it were better to reserve the term for the four players, and call the section of the green upon which they play "the space," which, as it happens, is not used otherwise in connection with the game.

Four players, we have just said, constitute

a rink. These are called, in Bowler's parlance, the leader, the second, the third man, and the skip, director, or driver. The last-named is the general, and upon his skill, strategy, and play will depend the success or failure of the rink. He is commonly blamed, and perhaps on the whole justly, for failure, and commonly praised, and perhaps on the whole too exclusively, for success. At any rate, it is more probable that failure has resulted from his defective strategy than from collapse of all four players, while success is generally due to good play by one or more of his colleagues as well as to generalship and play on his part. However, he is in charge of the rink, and his men must obey him implicitly. Even when the event proves to demonstration that the driver's judgment was at fault; even though the player in the act of play feels sure that the instruction with which he is about to comply is a grave mistake, still the skip must be obeyed at all costs. In the rink game there is no room for the individualist, for it presupposes combination for a given object which has been thought out by the skip and towards which each of his men is expected to devote his best skill and attention. This is, indeed, the beauty of the game. The building up of an end ought to prove a subject of interest to all four men engaged in it.

None of the quartet plays a more important part than the first man, or

LEADER.

For the skip can initiate no plan of campaign until he has obtained a bowl that is likely either to count or to be of value to him in the development of a scheme. The first thing the leader must do is to throw the jack. He will, of course, throw one to which either he or his rink may be partial. Nay more, he must watch the length of jack that his rival prefers—it may be a baby one, it may be a full-length,—so that he may throw one of the reverse length when he has the privilege. The skip should not presume to direct his leader, who has, indeed, been selected for the position because of his customary skill in playing to a clear jack. I have little faith in any skip who interferes at this early stage, yet I have seen one actually show his leader both the hand and the ground! That is playing the grandfather with a vengeance. The leader, if an experienced player, will always do best whom his skip leaves perfectly untrammelled. He knows as well as the skip does that the only man he has to beat is the leader opposed to him, and he should be permitted to do this without let or hindrance. The leader must play to the jack, must go all the way to it, on no account falling short in either draw. He will try to lie on the jack, either immediately in front or immediately behind. Should he succeed in gaining one of these positions with his first bowl, he will probably have no difficulty in securing the other with his second. Even if the leader be somewhat too strong with both bowls, no great harm will have been done. For any shortcomings in respect of finer or closer play can always be made good by the

Second Player.

Some Bowlers affect to regard this position as derogatory. That is all nonsense. Of course every Bowler believes himself to be either a born skip or a born lead, but, granting this, every player in a rink is " cast " for a definite *rôle*; each man's responsibility is as great as his fellow's, and he is expected (by England, or his club—it doesn't matter which) to do his duty. It is quite true that if a skip has a man of whose play he is a little in doubt, he will place him in the second line, because in that position he can do himself most justice and the rink least harm. Hence this player has been called the " soft second," solely for the reason just given.

The fact is you cannot play more than four men in a rink, and one of them has got to be

THE SECOND'S RESPONSIBILITY 63

second. A player who feels slighted at being required to fill this place is either an indifferent sportsman, or else overlooks a most important consideration. Let him forget for the nonce that he is one of four, and assume that he is playing second in a pairs competition, and he must surely realise that his position is both honourable and responsible. This, in truth, is the view which every second should take and, so regarded, it will be evident that he has been assigned a post in which he may render signal service to his skip and his side.

As a rule, the skip will begin his course of active instruction with the second player, of whom as much may be demanded as of the leader—and possibly even more. For his may be the privilege of compensating for any deficiency of the first man's play. The second should therefore be equally versed in drawing to the actual jack, or to a spot on the green which the skip will indicate, and to which he will be requested to play *as to the jack itself*. Take the case mentioned of the leader having played both of his bowls too forcibly. The skip has two back " woods," but no shot. The second may be bidden either to draw to the jack on a given hand, or carry the jack towards the back bowls: the situation (which is by no means rare) will afford any player a legitimate chance of distinguishing himself.

To the second is deputed the duty of keeping the score of his rink. The score is agreed at every end, and the second of the side that has won the head, in English play, calls out to his skip (who is at the other end of the green) the score and the number of ends played. This duty must never be neglected; otherwise, should his side be falling behind, the skip, in ignorance of the score, might leave his effort to save the situation till it were too late: in Scotland the skip may inquire at intervals as to "how goes the game?"

Ordinarily a match comprises twenty-one ends, but it may be agreed to play twenty-five or other number. The second will be careful to note that a tie end, while yielding no point to either side, nevertheless counts an end and must be marked "tie"; while a case of "no end"—as when the jack has been driven out of bounds, or a bowl has been "burned" and the opposite party claims a fresh head—of course, does not count. The number of rinks taking part in a match is commonly three or four, but it may be as few as one, or as many as six or eight (or the full number, whatever this be, which the green will accommodate). Four rinks a-side, however, provide a very excellent game and do not impose unduly upon the hospitality of the entertaining club. It is usual either to interrupt a match at "half-

THE SKIP'S DEPUTY

time" for refreshment, or for the home player to take his rival to the canteen at the psychological moment. I think the latter the better plan. Indeed, I have seen a rink fall to pieces after an interval for drinks, not in consequence of the copiousness of the draughts or the potency of the liquor, but for the more prosaic reason that they have lost their "feel" of the green and "sight" of the jack, and their poor play renders them panic-stricken.

To resume the main subject, the

THIRD MAN

ought to be almost if not quite as good a man as the skip, for whom, in point of fact, he deputises when occasion demands (as when the skip goes to the mat to play, or leaves the green for a glass of ginger beer). On this account he generally stands at the jack along with the skip, so that the two may exchange views about any situation that may call for exceptional play. This custom originated in Scotland, but, on the whole, it has little to recommend it. If the skip is worthy of his position, he should not need a counsellor; if he is inferior to the third man, the two ought to change places in the next match. Repeated consultations waste time and do not always result in agreement. Moreover, the skip may, at any juncture, summon a player from the mat to look at the lie of the " woods " before delivering his bowl. What may be required of the third man when his turn shall come it is impossible to conjecture, as it entirely depends upon the then aspect of things. His all-round proficiency having been postulated, he is expected to be equal to any emergency. He may have a " soft thing on," or the position may be so desperate as to make the highest possible demand on his resourcefulness. One point is, therefore, evident : the third man must have plenty of nerve.

The Skip,

driver, or director of a rink, is not put into that post casually. No Bowler should be elected to serve as skip excepting for specific reasons patent to his fellows. Though he fills the position of an autocrat he must not wield his power autocratically. He may not be, and often is not the best player in the club, but he should be there or thereabouts : let us say, among the best. He ought to know the laws by heart and be able to cite the rubric for or against any disputed point that may crop up during play. He must be a thorough general, quick to seize possibilities, sagacious to conceal his plan as long as may be from his adversary, and of sound judgment so that he may settle promptly the best line of play at any crisis. He must be a man of the world and have a sympathetic knowledge of human nature. Peevish, cross-grained, ill-tempered, dour men are by nature unqualified for a post in which tact and the gift of managing men are supremely essential.

Occasionally a skip may notice one of his men more interested in an adjoining rink or game than in his own, and will be justified in quietly checking such "slackness," but to lecture or hector a man " before folk " is the blundering of a bully. When a diplomatic skip has set a player a task which the latter doesn't like, or if he is not himself quite sure of the best possible shot to attempt, he will always allow the man a chance of offering a counter-opinion. " What do you see ? " he asks, and should the skip believe the alternative plan sufficiently promising he will sanction it. The young player should not stand in awe of his skip, but regard him as a guide, philosopher, and friend, and solicit advice and instruction whenever he feels the need of it.

W. W. Mitchell set a high value on the skip's knowledge of human nature. " Never disparage the play of your own side," he wrote, " but rather try to find something to commend in every bowl [save a really bad one: for indiscriminate praise is worthless and depreciates eulogy of shots that deserve approval]—'the very length,' 'well-greened,' 'a good guard,' 'the best back one,' 'the very place,' 'you for a player!' 'you have played before!' etc. etc." He goes on to say that the play of opponents may be spoken of lightly, provided it be done genially by way of banter. I do not endorse this opinion, if only because the skip has nothing to do with the play of the other side, and should leave it to be dealt with by the rival skip. Nevertheless, while encouraging his men by discreet praise of good shots, the skip should not be too demonstrative. A noisy skip is a nuisance, not perhaps so much to his own rink, who have been broken in to his eccentricities, as to players in adjoining rinks, who might be disturbed by wild yells or ludicrous gestures.

As last player grave responsibility rests upon the skip, whose last bowl may have to avert disaster in the shape of a heavy adverse score, to save, or to win a game. Being the tactician of his rink, he not only closely superintends his own men's play and watches the vicissitudes of every end, but also keenly observes the plan and play of the rival general. Years of play may not make a competent skip, for much depends on the man apart from the player, upon his gift of strong, swift and sure decision, upon his handling of his fellows. In

THE SKIP'S OPPORTUNITY 69

short, the ideal skip, like the poet, is born and not made.

Exactly what he may have to achieve when his turn comes, it is impossible to forecast here. He may have to accomplish a perfect draw to prevent a large score on the other side. This will seldom be an easy task, because it is very unlikely that the draw will be clear on either hand after twelve or fourteen bowls have been despatched towards the jack. Sometimes, however, a port may be negotiable by a fine draw; sometimes it may be possible to reach the jack by a cannon from another bowl, the " chap and lie " of Bowlers' jargon, conveyed, in turn, from the roaring game; sometimes the first place may be gained by a " follow-through " shot by drawing rather heavily upon a bowl that blocks the path, and forcing it up the green, while the player's own bowl continues to run towards the jack. But it is idle to pursue surmise further.

One stroke falls to the lot of the skip pretty often and that is the drive. It comes to him, because he must never allow an earlier player to fire. A hostile bowl on the jack seems to have an irritating effect upon certain skips, who do not scruple to bid, it may be, the second man " pick off this bowl." The position can be more effectually dealt with otherwise than by sacrificing at least one bowl of the skip's side. In driving the bowl is well set up in the player's hand and delivered with enough strength to overcome or destroy the bias for the moment. If the skip *must* fire, he will not hesitate to do so, for to be in two minds about the policy of driving is to invite failure. But do not fire at random; let the target be clearly sighted, lest the driver strike the wrong object—with sad results. Firing demands a keen eye and sure hand, and is almost forbidden if the skip have neglected to call for back bowls from one or other of his players. No skip should make a habit of driving, since excessive resort to it inevitably spoils his hand for the finer shades of play frequently necessary towards the close of an end. Having to kill the bias of his bowl when firing, a skip who glories in his prowess as a rider, unconsciously falls into the mode of drawing with narrow bias and ultimately becomes useless unless he abandon the error of his ways.

Probably the deadliest and most brilliant shot the skip may have to execute is to carry the jack to a cluster of bowls of his own men. Such a position, however, should seldom arise, because no alert skip will allow his rival to accumulate a number of bowls at any spot where they might conceivably count against him, and will rather take the precaution to mix two or

TRAILING AND GUARDING

three bowls of his own amongst the others. Still, the opportunity does occur, and the skip who is able to take full advantage of the trail may reap a rich harvest.

Upon the question of protecting a shot by guarding it with another bowl, there is some difference of opinion, although there is a consensus that it is feeble policy to do so in the ordinary development of an end. A guard posted early is a bowl wasted. But there are exceptions to every rule. Suppose the jack driven into the ditch and a bowl not a " toucher " on the brink, become shot in consequence of the fresh complexion put upon the lie of the woods by the carry, it would be legitimate to endeavour to guard this, since it should be easier to play a defending bowl rather than try for a second shot, with the chance of being a trifle too strong and sending the shot into the ditch—and the fresh bowl, too. When the skip wishes a block he will issue express orders to that effect, and indicate where he wishes the bowl to rest: otherwise no Bowler should attempt to play a guard of his own accord.

After the skip has played the last bowl of an end, the score is agreed and entered on the card, the skip meanwhile laying the mat on the bank. Should any measurement be necessary, this will be done by a player on each side (in Australian practice the third men are nominated to this duty, and this is to be recommended), the other players watching that the measuring is carried out with scrupulous fairness. The mere fact of such a test's being necessary implies that there is little to choose between the bowls in question, and the string held not so taut to one bowl as to another might give the shot to the latter, when perhaps there was actually a tie. When the bowls are near enough to enable mechanical measurers (such as callipers) to be employed, these are always the most satisfactory, since they can be very accurately adjusted and cannot easily be tampered with. In the case of measurement, there must be absolute agreement on both sides before either bowl is disturbed.

Had I not seen too many instances to the contrary, I should not have presumed to counsel the skip to win modestly and to lose with temper. It seems as difficult for some men to lose with dignity as to win with equanimity. Some skips have a good " conceit of themselves "; the vanity of some is amusing, that of others offensive. Every failure is " hard lines," every success is self-lauded to the skies, and their impatience of well-intended criticism too often takes the form of a sneer at the " wonderful play on the banks." Crowing over a victory is ill-mannered, while to sulk, or betray annoyance at defeat is ill-natured. The skip of evenly-balanced mind is sure to congratulate his rival upon a victory well won, and if the latter cannot find something kindly to say of his opponent, he must either be inordinately vain or the play must have been really poor.

Scottish Bowlers were the inventors of one of the most conspicuous features of the rink game, namely, "touchers" and their corollaries, "ditchers," and the vitality of the jack wherever it may be carried or driven within the limits of the space, until the end is played out. These three features have even been erected into a triad of fetishes. A toucher is a bowl which, in the course of its original career, has hit or touched the jack —the merest almost imperceptible brush will suffice. It must be gently marked with a chalk cross by the skip as soon as it has come to a standstill: unless it is so marked before the second next bowl is delivered it cannot be claimed as a toucher. Although it may have collided with one or more bowls before it touches the jack, it is still a toucher; but should a bowl be forced on to the jack by another bowl, such a bowl is not a toucher. A toucher must be active, not passive. In virtue of being a toucher, it is alive until the close of the head, no matter where it may lie within the limits of the space, even if it run into the ditch in its original course, or be driven into it by a succeeding bowl, directly or indirectly.

It is difficult to see how touchers advantage the game. A leader playing to a clear jack often succeeds in touching the mark, and, at this stage of the game, the feat is one of commonplace dexterity, demanding no special reward on its merits. But it is by no means certain that this may not have been the *fons et origo* of the feature, for W. W. Mitchell asserts that, in the infancy of touchers, the bowl was marked not by chalk but in a " more primitive mode." The player, he says, " felt proud to hear his driver exclaim, ' That one deserves a spittle,' and accordingly it had this, by way of distinction, put upon it." To be spat upon is universally regarded as a sign of the most undisguised contempt; but Bowls is unique in affording an example of an expectoration being accepted *honoris causa*, as if it were a medal at an International Exhibition!

There is even a certain injustice in touchers that savours of poor sportsmanship. Suppose, for instance, the leader has delivered his bowl with unnecessary strength and that it just brushes the jack and then runs into the ditch, it may be, some eighteen feet farther on. That was really a bad bowl, but the skip, with all the gravity imaginable, stoops to decorate it with a cross. Of course, this bowl might become most valuable in the event of the jack's being driven to keep it company in the ditch; but few skips would discover in the fact of a leader's bowl lying in the ditch, a clue to building up the end on such lines as to make the bowl count in the score. A toucher in the ditch can only be disturbed by another toucher's coming into contact with it and altering its position, or by the jack being driven against it in the course of play.

"Ditchers" and the "live jack" follow as a matter of course from touchers. For this reason all dead bowls—those which have run into the ditch without touching the jack or have been driven into it, and are hence called ditchers—must be removed to the bank as soon as they fall into the ditch.

Actually the "live jack" is another questionable feature. It is conceivable that a leader might deliberately try to drive or carry the jack into the ditch at every head. In so doing he would be acting within the letter of the law as well as in a mischievous and perverse spirit. That such a gross abuse could take place under the statutes shows that the doctrine of the "live jack" transcends the bounds of legitimate sportsmanship.

Advocates of the Scottish view maintain that the maxim " the jack never dies " (within the bounds of the space) penalises indiscriminate firing by rendering the effects of a smashing bowl uncertain. Why, they urge, should a beautiful head, the result of high-class play, be ruined, perhaps time after time, by wanton driving ? But the " live jack " offers no such guarantee, and may, indeed, rather be regarded as placing a premium upon " going it blindly " and driving merely " on spec." The consequence of a riding bowl cannot be estimated beforehand with any approach to accuracy, and *may* do greatest damage to the rider's own side. Besides, the proper way to protect well-placed bowls from being dislodged is either to guard them or, preferentially, to have one or two bowls behind the jack. It is not that the " live jack " stultifies delicate and skilful play that this feature is fundamentally objectionable, but that it not only introduces into a scientific game the element of chance but also gives all the compensation, or a disproportionate share of it, to the lucky bowl that works the havoc. The old English practice of ignoring touchers and ditchers and treating the end as " no end " whenever the jack was driven into the ditch was more sportsmanlike and more logical. To adopt this view would lead to the disappearance of the ditch; but, after all, it is only by an arbitrary juggling with words, or a kind of legal verbal violence, that the ditch is not a ditch but part and parcel of the green!

Many clubs elect a captain. There is an obvious convenience in the appointment of an officer who shall arrange matches and to whom all questions affecting the game and not the administration of the club may be referred; but custom is not uniform in this respect and many clubs get on very well without a captain, electing in his stead a certain number of skips for the season and a small match committee. But when a club desires a captain, let the members choose no *roi fainéant*. A strong captain will not shirk responsibility with power, but will not look at the office otherwise. Such a captain will select the skips and, in consultation with them, compose the match teams, and arrange the matches for the ensuing season. To the proper captain the members' confidence will certainly go out without stint, but they have a clear right to expect him to attend the green constantly, in order to study the play of members, to coach them when necessary, to watch " on-coming " talent, to discourage favouritism or cliquism, and always " to play the game."

CHAPTER V

THE POINTS GAME AND FIXED JACK

Playing with the Head—Infinite Variety in Bowls—THE GAME OF POINTS—Preparation of the Green—Rules of the Competition — DRAWING — Disposition of the Plan — GUARDING—Arranging the Ground—TRAILING—The Prepared Green—DRIVING—To encourage Proficiency in Drawing—FIXED JACK—Plan of the Green—Duties of the Starter—The Marker and the Score—The Carried Jack—Line Bowls—Method of Play.

SINCE the complete Bowler "plays with his head," the result of brain-work is seen in almost every end in the kaleidoscopic changes that necessitate, on the instant, corresponding changes in defence or attack. The resources of his art are not easily exhausted: there is no such thing as finality in its technics. But whatever the Bowler attempt, it must always be something definite. Haphazard, nondescript play is especially futile. Before the bowl leave his hand the Bowler should have a particular purpose in view and, if he accomplish it, this will be due to applied logic as well as to skilful manipulation of his " wood." Discomfited he will often be, but failure ought

THE FINESSE OF BOWLS

never to be caused by playing purely at a venture. If he cannot achieve his object directly, he may succeed by means of contingent or secondary methods, such as the follow-through, " chap and lie," double-cannon, the guard, the drive, the drag, the trail, and other shots.

Accordingly, no Bowler may be deemed expert who cannot execute both the intricate and the straightforward shots; and, in order to promote efficiency in the *finesse* of Bowls the game of

POINTS

has been introduced. By the nature of the case it can only be played with advantage on greens of good quality, and the finer the better. It illustrates four separate shots the necessity for one or other of which is certain to arise in every match. These are Drawing, Guarding, Trailing, and Driving. For the first three kinds some slight preliminary preparation of the far end of the playing space is necessary, and the head should be not less than 33 yards from the mat, and the jack should be placed at least three yards from the top ditch (in Guarding, the upper jack should be so stationed). The stance of jack and bowls in the prearranged head should be marked on the turf with a " dab " of whitewash, so that they may be readily restored to their original positions in the event of their being dislodged, as will often occur.

Every player uses four bowls, played on the fore and back hand alternately, change of bowl after the start not being sanctioned. In those cases in which all four competitions are being played the same day, one rink being reserved for each section, every candidate makes two rounds of the green, playing four shots at each point; in those cases where a separate evening is given up to each section, he plays his four bowls twice. Ties are settled by playing in each section one bowl on the fore hand and one on the back. Preliminary practice—one shot on the fore and one on the back hand—is permitted in Drawing only. The marker stands at the jack to declare and record the value of each shot that scores, and he may also, if requested, act as umpire.

In DRAWING, three concentric circles of one, two, and three feet radii from the centre tee on which the jack is placed must first be described with whitewash on the green. Then, at a distance of fifteen feet from the jack, and in front of it, two bowls are placed in a horizontal line five feet apart, so that were the line dividing them drawn (which it is not) a perpendicular line from the tee would bisect it. The player's bowl must pass outside of the

DRAWING 81

stationary bowls without touching them and then come to rest within one of the circles. If it lie within the one-foot circle three points will

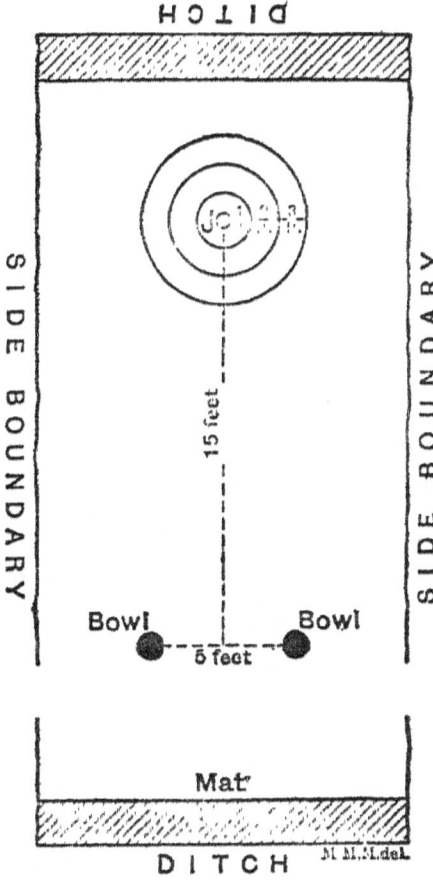

THE HEAD SET FOR DRAWING.

be scored, within the two-foot circle two, and within the three-foot circle one. The highest possible score is twelve. If a bowl rest upon the circumference of a circle, its value will be ascertained by the marker's applying, as the case may be, a three-, two-, or one-foot rule to the centre of the bowl and jack, and assigning the score of the circle within which the major portion of the bowl is found to lie.

For GUARDING, several lengths of strong white thread are required, two of eleven feet long, two of ten and two of nine, these being arranged as shown in the diagram. The two longest are pinned down on the green, at the far end, in vertical lines about twelve feet from the ditch and six inches apart from each other. On each side of these the ten-foot thread is then fastened to the turf at a distance of six inches from the eleven-foot thread and one foot lower down the green. On each side of the ten-foot threads the nine-foot thread is similarly secured, six inches apart and one foot still lower down the green. Then one jack is laid at the head of the middle space, exactly in the centre, and another jack at the foot of this space and also in the centre, the two being twelve feet apart in a vertical line. Standing at the mat, the player bowls on the fore and back hand alternately with a view to laying the bowl, when dead, on the centre space or either of the side spaces. Should the bowl lie in the middle space three points are given, two points for a bowl in either adjoining space, and one point for a bowl in the outermost.

GUARDING 83

Thus twelve is the highest possible score, if all four bowls lie in the middle. The bowl must, in every case, be quite clear of the thread. If

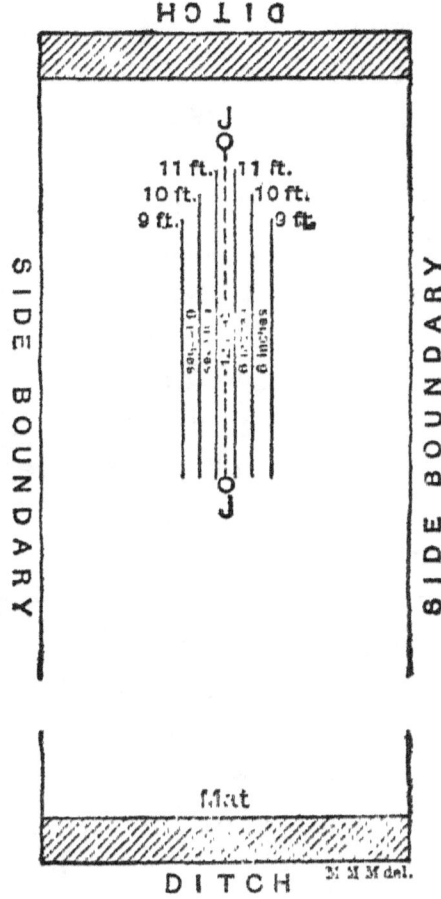

THE HEAD ARRANGED FOR GUARDING.

a bowl touch the top jack—the one being guarded, it will not count at all. If it seem certain that the running bowl will touch the front jack, this should be temporarily lifted.

TRAILING is the section of the Points game which is most worthy of attention. It demands beautiful play and is often extremely effective in a match. In arranging the head it is necessary to place two bowls at the far end of the green at a distance of three feet from each other and exactly horizontal, and then to draw with whitewash, or lay down in strong white thread, a straight line from bowl to bowl across the back and front faces. A jack is then placed just in front of the front line, exactly in the middle and equidistant from each bowl. Behind the bowls a semicircle is drawn in whitewash on the turf with a radius of nine feet from the jack. The head as finally prepared is shown in the diagram. The Bowler is required to trail the jack, his own bowl accompanying or " hugging " it, between the stationary bowls over both of the horizontal lines, into but not outside of the semicircle. If he succeed he will score three points. But if he only trail the jack over the back line without sending his own bowl over, or if the jack be trailed over the front line only, his bowl crossing the back, he will score two points. If his bowl pass between the jack and the stationary bowls over the back line without touching the jack; or if it touch the jack and do not carry it over the front line but itself cross the back line; or if it trail the

TRAILING

jack across the front line without itself passing it, he will score one point. Twelve points is the maximum score for one round. The

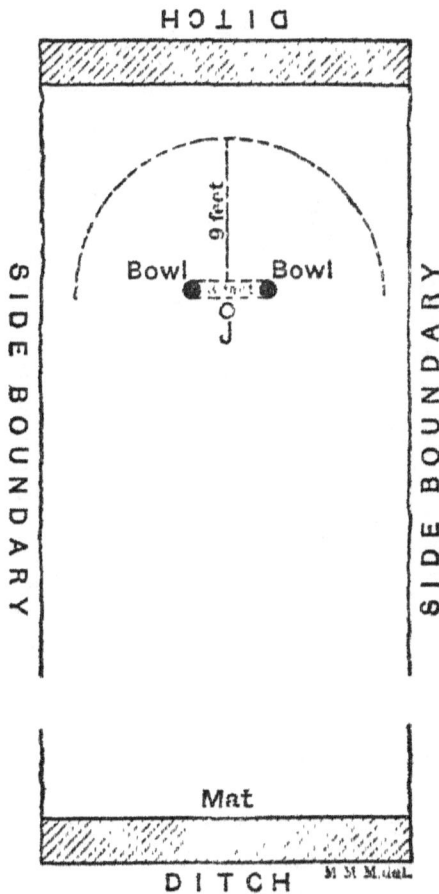

THE HEAD PREPARED FOR TRAILING.

scoring is very partial, for the trailing really done in the exercises for which two points and one point are allowed is either defective or infinitesimal. By comparison the player who

86 THE POINTS GAME

trails perfectly is inadequately recompensed with three points. In all three exercises the player's bowl must not touch the stationary

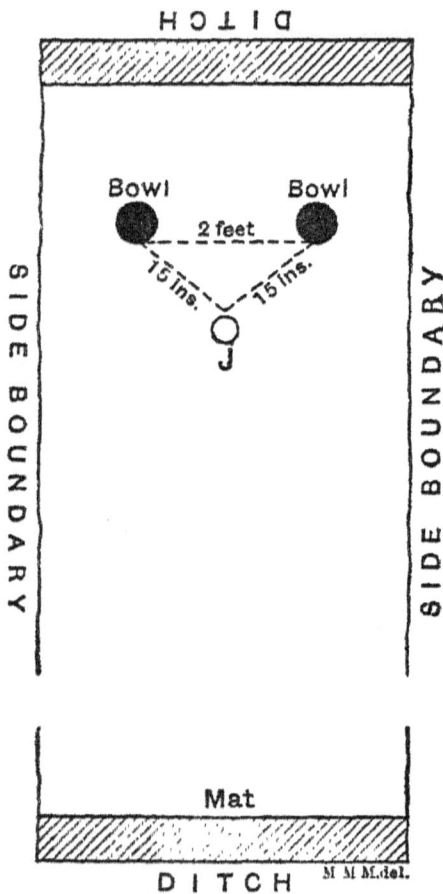

THE HEAD MADE READY FOR DRIVING.

bowls, nor must the played bowl and trailed jack travel beyond the semicircle.

All that is needed for the exercise of DRIVING is to lay down two bowls, two feet apart in a horizontal line, and, in front of them a jack, fifteen inches apart from each, occupying thus the position of the apex of an inverted pyramid, as shown in the diagram. If the player drive the jack between the bowls into the ditch and his own bowl run thither also he will score three points; two points will be allowed if he shift the jack without sending it between the bowls into the ditch, into which his own must run; and one point will be gained if, his own bowl ultimately running into the ditch, he touch the jack without moving it, or pass between the jack and the stationary bowls, although he has done no driving whatever! In all three cases the player's bowl must not touch either stationary bowl. The highest possible score is twelve points.

As each competitor in the Points game must go twice round the green—or, in the alternative, play twice at each exercise,—and the maximum score in each section is twelve, the highest possible aggregate is ninety-six points.

With the object of encouraging proficiency in the art of drawing, another exercise, known as the

Fixed Jack

game, has been devised. It is not uncommon, because it may be practised on greens that are not quite up to the high standard demanded

THE FIXED JACK

by the whole of the Points game. As it monopolises all the green a competition is usually held only once a month or so.

During the forenoon the groundman will lay out the green according to a plan prepared for him. A green set for twelve jacks is shown in the diagram on pp. 218, 219. The number must depend upon the size of the green, but the larger the number that can be accommodated the better, provided that the rinks are not too closely packed.

Before play all the mats are laid on the banks and the jacks in the ditch, opposite to their respective stances. The tee for each jack is plainly marked with whitewash and around this, as centre, three concentric circles are described having radii of one foot, two feet, and three feet. The order of play should be balloted for three days before and exhibited on the notice-board. Time defaulters are sent down to the last places, though in important contests disqualification is the penalty. In the event of a heavy entry the competition may be extended over one or more days. The starter officiates as master of the ceremonies.

Every competitor must provide his own marker. Usually the late starters act in this capacity, the earlier ones being in honour bound to reciprocate. The markers are supplied with identical scoring cards, which

METHOD OF SCORING 89

they sign before returning to the secretary. Every bowl lying within the one-foot circle counts three, within the two-foot circle two, and within the three-foot circle one. If a player's first bowl knock the jack off its perch into any of the circles and the bowl also rest in a circle, the score of the latter circle will be allowed; but if the jack be driven outside of the circles no score will be reckoned, even though the bowl lie within a circle. The jack must be replaced before the second bowl is delivered, and, if the like be repeated, similar procedure will be followed. It is better, however, to authorise the marker to lift the jack altogether when he sees the bowl will hit it, and then replace it after the bowl has passed. A bowl lying on a circumference line takes the score of the circle within which the greater portion of it lies. Thus, if the major part project outside of the periphery of circle three, the marker will allow no score; but should any line divide the bowl equally, half of the combined circle values will be scored.

Usually when a bowl has been scored (if it be a counter) it is removed, but it may be agreed beforehand that the bowl must lie until the second has been played. Whichever method be adopted, it must be applied throughout, but the former is preferable. As every player uses two bowls and the highest possible

THE FIXED JACK

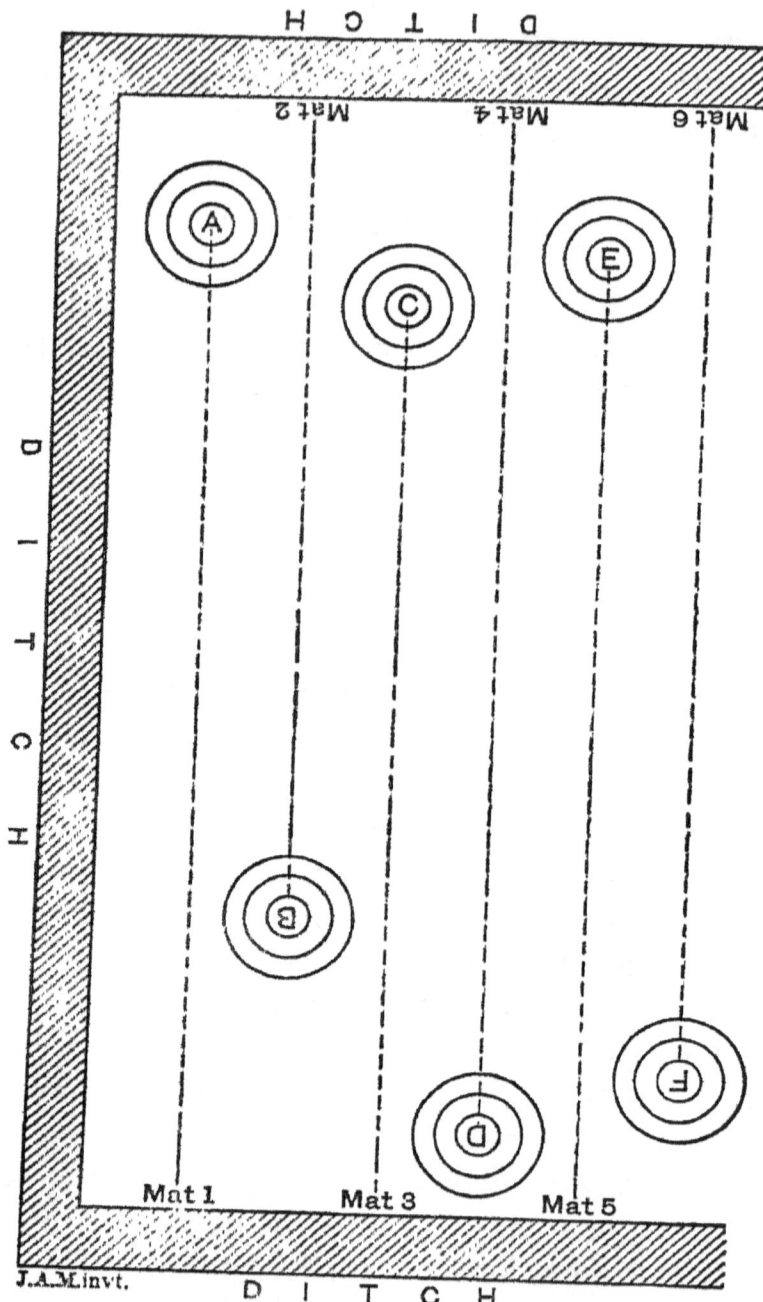

Green Set for Twelve Jacks in the Fixed Jack Game;

THE FIXED JACK

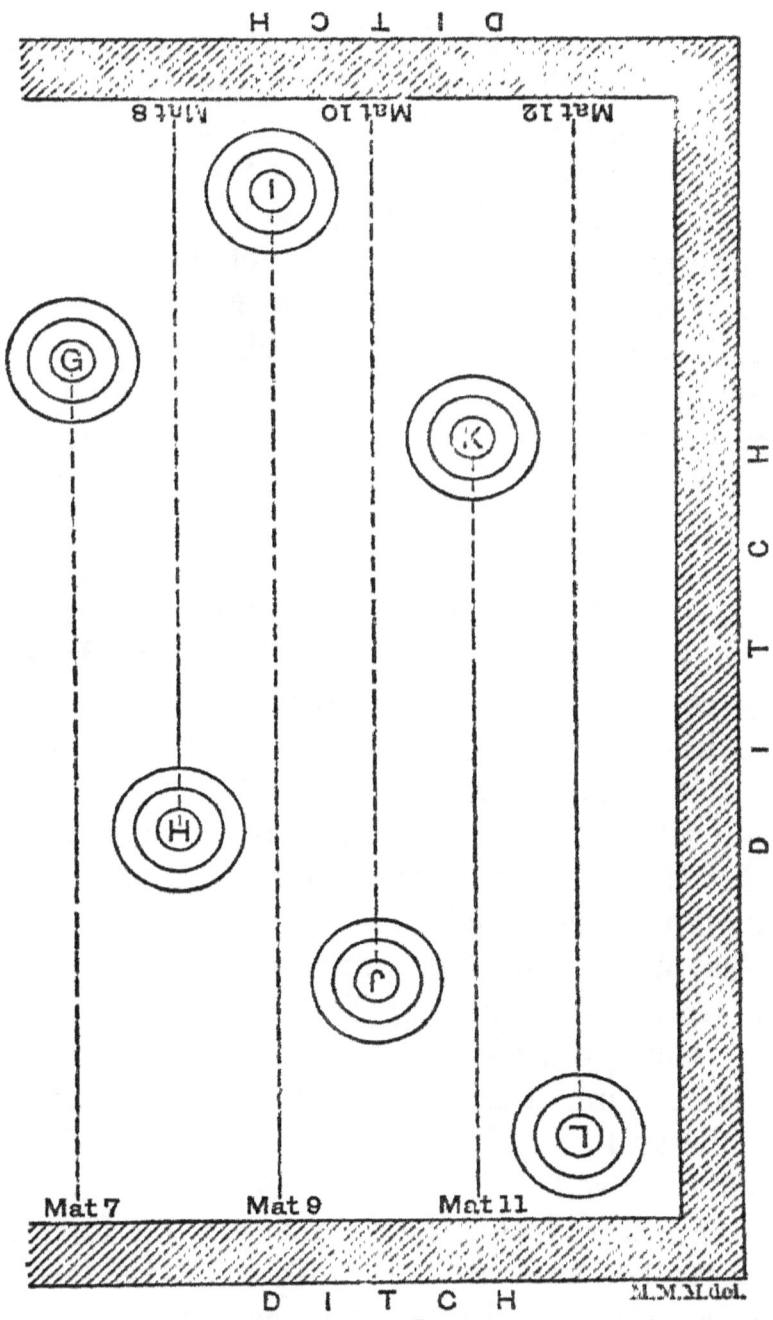

A, B, ETC., INDICATE THE POSITION OF THE JACKS.

THE FIXED JACK

score at a jack is six, the highest aggregate for a round of twelve jacks is seventy-two.

One round suffices for a green set for eight jacks and upwards, two rounds for a green set for six jacks, which must be taken as the minimum, if the competition is not to be robbed of all value. For it is of the essence of the Fixed Jack game that the jacks shall be of varying length, two jacks of like length in succession being forbidden. Each mat is placed in position and afterwards removed to the bank by the player, while each jack is placed *in situ* and then removed to the ditch by the marker. Competitors must take their turn at the starter's summons. It would be an advantage to require one bowl to be played on the fore hand and the other on the back; but without a hard and fast rule to this effect, competitors are free to follow their own sweet will. No preliminary practice must be allowed. This is very essential.

Sharply on time, the starter despatches No. 1, simultaneously warning No. 2 to get ready. No 1. then proceeds to Mat 1 and lays the mat, his marker meanwhile having taken his stand at circle A and placed the jack on the tee. No. 1 having played both bowls and the marker having entered the score (if any), the former restores the mat to the bank and the latter the jack to the ditch. The competitor next

THE GAME IN PROGRESS

goes to Mat 2 and the marker to circle B, where a similar routine is pursued. But as soon as the candidate goes to Mat 3 the starter sends off No. 2 at Mat 1 with *his* marker at circle A, and so on with the remaining players, a constant succession of competitors being maintained until the close, at intervals of two jacks from each other. When the rivalry is in full blast, the green presents an exceedingly animated appearance.

CHAPTER VI

THE LAWS OF BOWLS

The Twenty Laws of the Game—I. Rinks, or Divisions of the Green—II. Bowls: Size and Bias—III. Size of the Jack—IV. Conditions of a Game—V. Rink, or Team of Players—VI. Skips, or Drivers—VII. The Mat—VIII. Throwing the Jack—IX. Movement of the Jack and of Bowls—X. Jack, or Bowl Rebounding—XI. Jack, or Bowl Burned—XII. Touchers—XIII. Ditchers—XIV. Possession of the Rink—XV. Result of Head—XVI. Changing Bowls—XVII. Objects on the Green—XVIII. Leaving the Green—XIX. Single-handed Games—XX. Onlookers.

WE are now able to study profitably the Laws of the level-green game of Bowls, which were drafted by a sub-committee of the Scottish Bowling Association and are issued—with such revision as may be adopted from time to time —under its sanction. They govern the rink, single-handed, and pairs games alike and are, in the main, recognised throughout the world by all clubs in possession of greens of adequate size and quality. The laws are twenty in number, many of them being divided into clauses. In several instances, too, the Scottish Bowling Association has annotated

THE RINK, OR PLAYING SPACE 95

them. These annotations are, in the following pages, placed within square brackets. I have added, in certain cases, comments of my own, and these are distinguished by the letters N.B. prefixed. The salient part of each law has been printed in black type, whenever it has seemed helpful to do so.

LAWS OF THE GAME

(*As drafted by the Scottish Bowling Association*)

LAW I.—RINKS, OR DIVISIONS OF THE GREEN

1. The green shall be divided into spaces, called **rinks, not less than 19 nor more than 21 feet in width,** numbered consecutively, the centre of each rink being marked on the bank at each end by a pin or other device, and the four corners of the rink by pins driven into the ditch. The side boundary of the rink shall stretch from bank to bank.

> [To prevent disputes, the pins at the opposite ends of the rink shall be connected by a linen thread drawn tightly on the surface of the green; and where practicable, the boundary pins of an outside rink shall be placed at least two feet from the side ditch. It is recommended that the bank be not less than 18 inches in height, with an angle from the green of not more than 120 degrees.]
>
> *N.B.*—By "pin" is meant an iron peg pointed to pierce the bank. It bears the number of the rink or playing space (1, 2, 3, 4, etc.) on an enamelled iron plate. The pegs which carry at the back a small metal cup (with a lid) for holding chalk are the best. The rinks should be divided by strong *thin* twine rather than thread,

drawn taut and laid dead flush with the turf, so that it shall not mar in the slightest degree the running of the bowl.

2. When a match is to be played, the numbers of the rinks shall be drawn at the green by the skips, or their representatives.

3. Ordinary games may be played on a rink mutually agreed upon.

N.B.—In such games "First come first served" usually determines the choice of rink. The laws should give members the right of choice of rink for championships, handicaps, and other special contests. In many, perhaps in most greens, all the rinks are not of equally good quality, and, in important contests particularly, it is desirable to allow a right of choice to the competitors. Players in occupation of a preferred space could not feel aggrieved at a request which carried the sanction of law behind it. Since the law is silent on the point, clubs should make the matter the subject of a byelaw.

LAW II.—BOWLS: SIZE AND BIAS

1. No bowl shall exceed **16½ inches in circumference, nor 3½ lbs. in weight, nor shall it have a less bias** than the standard bowl adopted by the Association.

N.B.—This law needs amendment in three particulars—(1), the minimum size, (2), the minimum weight, and (3), the minimum bias should be expressly stated. What *is* the bias of a standard bowl? What *is* the bias of a No. 3? Bowlers wishing to use bowls of larger bias than the standard are entitled to do so under this law.

2. Any bowl to which objection is taken shall be tested by comparison with a standard bowl of the Association, bearing the Association's stamp. Any **objection must be taken not later than the sixth head of a game.**

TESTING THE BIAS

In the case of a club match or competition, **the test shall at once be applied**, at the distance of 32 yards, by two referees appointed by the players; and if the referees disagree, they shall appoint an oversman. In the event of a bowl being declared of a less bias than the standard, the further use of it in that club match or competition shall not be allowed, and the player at fault shall, from the stage at which the game then stood, play with any bowl, conform to standard, selected for him by the referees or oversman, or forfeit the game. In the event of the game being so forfeited, the objecting rink or player shall, in addition to being declared winner, be entitled to add to its or his score one shot for such number of shots or heads as may still remain to be played.

In the case of a tournament, the bowl or bowls objected to by an opponent shall, at the conclusion of the game, be taken possession of by the Secretary of the tournament, who shall have the same forthwith tested by two of the *umpires of the tournament*, who are not members of the same club as either of the players, and who, if they cannot agree, shall call in another of the umpires, who must also be a neutral person, to determine whether the objection is *frivolous;* but if there be reasonable ground for doubt, the bowl or bowls shall at once be sent to one of the officers of the Association, to be tested by him. The officer shall test and return without delay all bowls thus sent to him, and shall also send to the Secretary of the tournament a written report of the result of the test. The decision of the umpires, oversman, or officer, as the case may be, shall be final. The objector shall lodge with the Secretary of the tournament the sum of ten shillings and sixpence, to cover the expense of testing, and to discourage frivolous objections, which sum shall be returned to him if his objection be sustained, and in that case the Secretary of the tournament shall recover said fee from the owner of the bowl or bowls before they are returned to him, and the competitor who used them shall be disqualified, and his opponent held as having won the tie.

[*Note.*—To facilitate the testing of bowls under the Law, the Association trusts that each constituent Club of the Association will provide itself with a standard bowl, made and stamped by one of its officers. Competitors in a public tournament are recommended to have their bowls tested and stamped beforehand.]

N.B.—Note the second sentence of the first section of the second clause. The reason why objection should be taken immediately cause for suspecting a bowl or bowls arises is obvious. If left to the end of a match, the umpire is bound to decline to entertain it, since it might be a mere pretext for a re-play. As evidence of good faith, therefore, an objection to an alleged unfair bowl, must be raised without the smallest delay. With reference to the S.B.A.'s Note, if clause 1, which sets forth the dimensions and weight of a bowl, were amended as proposed, and every bowl stamped with the number of its bias and the name of its maker, this precaution would go far to meet all requirements. It sometimes happens that bowls have their bias altered after they have left the manufacturer. In such case the new turner must obliterate the original stamp, and stamp the fresh bias on the bowls. The owner of the bowls must see that this is done, and the responsibility for the alterations in the bowls should be fastened upon him. Should it appear that, when re-turned, the bias has been reduced to less than No. 3 (defined as I have suggested), the turner should inform his customer and enter the new bias in his ledger with the date and name.

3. Markers.—In single-handed tournaments one marker only shall act in each game. **The marker may answer queries as to position of bowls and their distance from the jack, but shall not give directions to, consult with, nor assist either player as to the play.**

CONDITIONS OF A GAME

In no circumstances shall a marker display any object, in the hand or otherwise, for the guidance of a player. Markers shall be appointed by the Directors of the tournaments, Local Secretaries, or Umpires, whom failing, by the competitors themselves.

> *N.B.*—The first two sentences of this clause should also be held to govern club handicaps and other contests for prizes. It will be useful if the marker officiate as umpire as well as scorer. The scoring in a rink game is otherwise provided for.

LAW III.—SIZE OF THE JACK

The jack shall be about 2½ inches in diameter.

LAW IV.—CONDITIONS OF A GAME

1. A game may consist of any number of shots or heads, or may be played for any length of time, as previously agreed upon.

> *N.B.*—A game or match by time is open to such palpable abuse (which yet might be difficult of proof) that it should be forbidden by law.

2. When a game is stopped either by mutual arrangement or by the umpire after appeal to him, on account of darkness or the condition of the weather, or any other valid reason, it shall be resumed with the scores as they were when it was stopped.

3. When a match consists of more than one rink on each side, the total scores of the respective rinks shall decide the contest.

4. When a game consists of a stated number of heads, and there is only one rink on each side, should it be found when the given number of heads has been played that **the scores are equal, an extra head shall be played, and should**

the result again be a tie, another shall be played and so on until a decision is arrived at.

LAW V.—RINK, OR TEAM OF PLAYERS

1. A rink or team shall consist of four players, each playing two bowls, and called respectively leader or lead, second player, third player, and skip or driver, according to the order in which they play. It shall be in the power of either skip, before beginning a competition or tie, or on the resumption of an unfinished competition or tie, to require that not more than one trial head each way shall be played. **On the day of a competition or tie no player shall play on the green before such competition or tie starts, except in these trial heads.** Unless otherwise mutually agreed upon, the skips shall toss to decide which side shall play first, the winner of the toss to have the choice. In all subsequent heads the side which won the previous head shall play first. The leaders play their two bowls alternately, and so on, each pair of players in succession, to the end. The order of playing shall not be changed after the first head has been played. No one shall play until his opponent's bowl has come to rest; a bowl so played may be stopped by the opposing side and sent back to be played over again, and in the event of the bowl so played having moved the jack or a bowl, the opposing skip may allow the head to remain as it is after the bowl so played has come to rest or he may have the head begun anew.

2. **A bowl played by mistake** shall be replaced by the player's own bowl.

3. **When a player has played before his turn,** either skip may cause the bowl to be stopped in its course, and it shall be played in its proper order, but in the event of the bowl so played having moved either jack or bowl, the opposing skip may allow the head to remain as it is after

ABSENTEE PLAYERS

the bowl so played has come to rest, or he may have the head begun anew.

4. Any bowl which comes to rest within 15 yards from the front of the mat shall be counted dead.

5. If fewer than three players appear on either side, the game, so far as that side is concerned, shall not proceed, and the side at fault shall be held as having *failed to appear*, and shall forfeit the game. Should such forfeiture take place where more rinks than one from each club are concerned, and where the aggregate or average scores are to decide the contest, the scores of the remaining rinks only shall be counted, but such average shall, as a penalty in the case of the defaulting side, be arrived at by dividing the aggregate score by the number of rinks which should have played, and not, as in the case of the other club, by the number actually engaged in the game. In the absence of a single player, from one or both sides, in an ordinary club match or friendly game, the number of bowls shall be made up by the playing of odd bowls, these odd bowls being played by the first and second players, one each at each end. In a match for a trophy or other prize, where more rinks than one from each club are engaged, odd bowls must, in the absence of one of the players of any rink, be played in the manner above provided, but one-fourth of the total shots scored by such rink shall be deducted from its score at the end of the game. In a match for a trophy or other prize where a club is represented by only one rink, such rink must play with four men, all of whom must be *bona fide* members of the club. The failure of a full rink to appear, or the introduction of an ineligible player, shall cause the side at fault to forfeit the tie to the opposing side.

N.B.—The failure of a club or rink to appear cannot be too severely punished. Such dereliction of duty should be posted by the Association to which the defaulting club belongs. Since no club is required to enter for a competition save of its own free will, its undertaking should be fulfilled at all costs. A rink or rinks, as originally composed, may not (for good reasons) be available on the day appointed, but such a contingency can always be provided against by the nomination of a few reserves.

LAW VI.—SKIPS, OR DRIVERS

1. The skips shall have sole charge of their respective rinks, and their instructions must be obeyed by their own players.

2. The skip shall have the control of the play of his own side, but he may delegate this duty at any time during the game to a member of his rink.

> *N.B.*—This clause should explicitly state that the skip shall delegate his functions to the third player only. Such an instruction would prevent the squabbling that sometimes takes place among the other members of a rink in the skip's absence.

3. When not in the act of playing or directing, players must stand behind the jack or behind the mat, and as soon as a bowl is delivered the player directing, if in front of the jack, must retire behind it.

4. The last player shall remove the mat to the bank.

5. The two skips shall be judges of all disputed points, and, when they agree, their decision shall be final; if they cannot agree, the point shall be decided by the umpire previously appointed, whom failing, by a neutral person mutually chosen.

LAW VII.—THE MAT

1. At the beginning of the first head, the player to play first shall place the mat in the centre of the rink, not less than one yard from the ditch, and in all the subsequent

CONCERNING THE MAT

heads the leader of the rink which won the immediately preceding head shall place the mat as before stated. It shall, however, be in his option to lay the mat (1) at the place where the jack lay at the finish of the head, if that place be in the centre of the rink; (2) or if the place be not in the centre of the rink, then in a line straight across towards the centre thereof; (3) or between where the jack lay at the finish of the head and any place in the centre of the rink, so that the mat shall be not less than one yard from the ditch; but (4) if the jack, at the finish of a head, lies in the ditch, or less than one yard from it, the mat shall, in beginning the new head, be placed not less than one yard from the ditch, as above provided. On all occasions there must be a clear distance of not less than 27 yards between where the front of the mat is placed and the ditch at the opposite end.

2. The mat shall not be moved from its place till the head is finished, except when a jack is thrown into the ditch, **or outside the boundary of the rink,** or fewer than 25 yards from the mat placed more than a yard from the ditch behind. In any of these events the opposing player shall have the right of moving the mat backwards to a distance not less than one yard from the ditch, as above provided. Should a player, however, inadvertently move the mat from its place, the mat shall be restored to its original position. It is recommended that the size of the mat be not less than 22 by 14 inches, or thereabouts.

3. Each player, when delivering the bowl, must have one foot entirely on the mat. Should a player, after warning, persist in infringing this Rule, the umpire shall order his bowl to be stopped and removed to the bank.

LAW VIII.—THROWING THE JACK

1. The leader of the side which is to play first shall throw the jack from the mat.

2. **If the jack run into the ditch, or outside the**

boundary of the rink, at the first throw in a game, it shall, in the case of its running into the ditch, be placed two yards from it in the centre of the rink, and in the case of its being outside the boundary of the rink, it shall be straightened to the centre. If it be **thrown into the ditch or outside the boundary of the rink at any subsequent head, the opposing player shall throw it anew,** but shall not play first. When **thrown fewer than two yards from the ditch, the jack must be moved out to that distance.**

3. The jack **shall be thrown not fewer than 25 yards** from the front of the mat, and if it do not rest in the centre of the rink, it shall be moved straight across and placed in the centre. If it be thrown **fewer than 25 yards** either inside or outside the boundary of the rink, it shall be treated according to clause 2 of this law, and with the right to the opposing side to take back the mat, as provided in Law VII., clause 2.

4. If none of the foregoing laws has been transgressed, the jack shall be played to wherever it has been thrown; and after having been played to, it shall not be touched or interfered with in any manner otherwise than by the effects of the play, until the result of the head has been determined.

LAW IX.—MOVEMENT OF THE JACK AND OF BOWLS

1. **If the jack be driven into the ditch within the limits of the rink, its place shall be accurately marked, and it shall not be moved except by a toucher** (see Law XII., clause 6). **Should it be driven by a bowl in play wholly beyond the limits of the rink,** that is to say, over the bank, or past the side boundary of the rink, or into any opening or inequality of any kind in the bank (*e.g.*, a step cut in the bank), or on to any steps resting against the bank, *it shall be counted dead.*

THE CASE OF THE JACK

N.B.—Since the place of the jack in the ditch must be accurately marked (by drawing a circle in chalk around it), it should be lawful for the skip (or third man) to place it temporarily on the edge of the green, so that the bowler shall be able to obtain a clear sight of it, restoring it to the ditch as soon as the bowl has been greened. This, though sometimes done, is, under the letter of the law, not permissible, and I have known cases in which a claim for a "burned" jack—moved thus inadvertently—has been made. Such a claim is rather "sharp," but if persisted in must be upheld. It is legitimate for the skip to indicate the position of the jack in the ditch.

2. The foregoing rule as to being counted dead when driven beyond the limits of the rink shall likewise apply to a bowl, whether a *toucher* or not.

3. **Whenever the jack is "dead," the head shall in no case be counted a played head,** not even though all the bowls have been played.

4. **The jack, though driven to the side of the rink, if not wholly beyond its limits, may be played to on either hand, outside the limits of the rink.** A bowl played outside the limits of the rink which in its natural course (if not interfered with outside the rink) comes to rest within the limits of the rink shall not be counted dead, but any bowl so played, which, when it comes to rest, lies *wholly* outside the rink shall be counted dead.

5. In the event of the jack being broken, the head shall be begun anew.

LAW X.—JACK, OR BOWL REBOUNDING

If the jack run against the bank or a toucher in the ditch, and rebound on to the green, or after being played into the ditch be so operated upon by a toucher as to find its way on to the green again, it shall be played to in the same manner as if it had never been moved off the green. But a bowl similarly rebounding shall be counted dead, *unless it be a toucher*, and any bowl or jack moved in the rebound of a non-toucher shall be put back to its former position.

LAW XI.—JACK, OR BOWL BURNED

The term "burned" is applied to a jack or bowl which has been interfered with or displaced, otherwise than by a bowl in play.

JACK BURNED

1. *While in motion on the green.*
    If a jack while in motion on the green is burned—
    (a) By one of the players, the opposing side shall have the option of letting it lie where it rests, and playing the head out, or of beginning the head anew.
    (b) By a neutral person, or by a bowl belonging to a neutral person, the players shall come to an agreement as to its position, otherwise the head shall be begun anew.
2. *While in motion in the ditch.*
    If a jack while in motion in the ditch within the limits of the rink comes into contact with a bowl which is not a toucher, it shall lie where it rests, but such bowl must then be immediately removed from the ditch.
3. *While at rest.*
    If a jack while at rest on the green, or in the ditch, is burned—
    (a) By one of the players, the opposite side may replace it in its original position, or allow it to remain where it rests.

BURNED JACK AND BOWL

(b) By a neutral person, or by a bowl belonging to a neutral person, the sides shall come to an agreement as to its position, otherwise the head shall be begun anew.

Bowl Burned

1. *While in motion.*
    A. If a bowl, during its original course, and before it has passed the jack, is burned—
      (a) By the side to which it belongs, the opposing side may—(1) declare it dead; (2) let it lie where it rests; or (3) have the head begun anew.
      (b) By an opponent, the player's side may claim—(1) to have it played over again; (2) to let it lie where it rests; or (3) to have the head begun anew.
      (c) By a neutral person, or by a bowl belonging to a neutral person, it shall be played over again.
    B. If a bowl which, in its original course, has passed the jack, whether it has touched the jack or not, and, being still in motion, is burned—
      (a) By the player's own side, it shall be counted dead, or, in the option of the opposing side, remain where it finally rests.

N.B.—The law is silent as to what shall be done with the jack which the "burned" bowl may have touched. Section (a) of clauses 1 and 3, strictly speaking, refers only to the burning of the jack by one of the players and not by his bowl. This point must be made here, because section (b) of these clauses deals with both the neutral person and his bowl. It is proper to punish the side to which the "burned" bowl belonged, but in touching the jack it may have materially affected the position of the other side. In such circumstances, the head ought to be started afresh.

THE LAWS OF BOWLS

(*b*) By an opponent, the player's side may choose to let it lie where it comes to rest, or to have the head begun anew.

(*c*) By a neutral person, or by a bowl belonging to a neutral person, it shall lie where it rests if both sides cannot agree as to where it would have come to rest.

(*d*) By contact with a non-toucher in the ditch, the "burned" bowl, if it be itself a toucher, shall be allowed to rest where it lies, and the non-toucher shall be moved to the bank.

C. If a bowl which had come to rest is afterwards set in motion by a bowl in play, and, while still moving, is burned—

(*a*) By the side to which it belongs, it shall be counted dead, or, in the option of the opposing side, remain where it finally rests.

(*b*) By an opponent, the side to which it belongs may choose to let it lie where it comes to rest, or place it where they consider it would probably have rested had it not been interfered with.

(*c*) By a neutral person, or a bowl belonging to a neutral person, it may be placed to the mutual satisfaction of both sides; where agreement cannot be attained, the bowl shall lie where it finally rests.

2. *While at rest.*

If a bowl while at rest is burned—

(*a*) By either side, it may be replaced by the opposite side, or, in the latter's option, be allowed to remain where it lies.

(*b*) By a neutral person, or by a bowl not in play, it should be replaced as near its original position as possible.

LAW XII.—TOUCHERS

1. A bowl which touches the jack during its original course on the green, **although previously it may have also touched one or more bowls,** is called a *toucher*, and is accounted in play wherever it rests, if within the rink, but should a bowl, after it has ceased running, fall over and touch the jack, *after another bowl has been delivered*, it is not to be accounted a toucher. **In no circumstances can a bowl become a toucher by touching the jack when the jack is in the ditch.**

2. Should a bowl which is not a toucher, and which has not been off the green, come to rest on the green after touching a jack or bowl which is a toucher in the ditch, it shall not be counted dead. In the event of its resting on a bowl in the ditch not a toucher, the bowl in the ditch must be removed, and should the bowl (not a toucher) so resting then fall into the ditch, it shall be counted dead.

3. **If a toucher run into the ditch** when played, or be driven into the ditch during the course of the subsequent play, **the place where it rests shall be marked,** but its position shall not be altered except by the action of another toucher or the jack.

4. **A toucher must be distinguished by a chalk or other distinct mark** put on it by the side to which it belongs. Unless it be marked before the second succeeding bowl is delivered, it is not to be accounted a toucher. **If the mark be not removed** from the bowl before it is played in the succeeding head, the opposing side may regard it as a *burned* bowl, and shall be entitled to remove it to the bank.

> *N.B.*—The object of prescribing a limit for the chalking is to prevent an improper claim for a toucher. That is the reason also why the mark must be wiped off before the bowl is played again. In the last sentence

of clause 4 "shall" should be substituted for "may." "May" is always bad.

5. If a bowl be moved *outwards* from the jack while being marked, it must remain as it is, but if it be moved *towards* the jack it must be restored to its original position.

6. Touchers may act on the jack, or touchers, in the ditch.

> *N.B.*—That is to say, a toucher is the only bowl that can act or operate upon the jack, or a toucher, or touchers in the ditch.

LAW XIII.—DITCHERS

1. A bowl which does not touch the jack in its original course on the green, and runs against the bank or into the ditch, or is driven into the ditch by the effects of the play, is called a *ditcher*, and shall be immediately removed to the bank by the side to which it belongs.

> *N.B.*—The skip, or third man, should see that this is promptly done. It is, in fact, imperative. Too many ditchers are allowed to remain in the ditch, through sheer carelessness.

2. Should a ditcher in any circumstances return to the green, it must be placed on the bank.

LAW XIV.—POSSESSION OF THE RINK

1. Possession of the rink shall belong to the side whose bowl is being played.

2. As soon as each bowl comes to rest, the possession of the rink is transferred to the other side, time being allowed for marking a toucher.

3. The side in possession of the rink for the time being must not be disturbed or annoyed by their opponents.

> *N.B.*—This clause is not particular enough to meet the case of those players who have a habit of making would-be funny remarks, or indulging in various antics

COUNTING AND MEASURING

which, whether so designed or not, may affect the play of some bowlers.

LAW XV.—RESULT OF HEAD

1. When the last bowl in a head stops running, half a minute shall elapse, if either side so require, before the shots are counted.

2. Neither jack nor bowls shall be moved until both sides are agreed as to the shots.

3. If a bowl requiring to be measured is resting on another bowl, which prevents its measurement, the best means available shall be taken to secure it in its position, whereupon the other shall be removed. The same course shall be followed when more than two bowls are involved.

4. No measuring shall be allowed until the head has been played out.

5. **When a tie for the first shot occurs, it shall, in a game of ends, be counted a played head.**

6. The duty of keeping the score, and of announcing the state of the game at the end of each head, should be assigned to the second player.

N.B.—This law should read more definitely thus:—
"The second player shall keep the score and shall announce to his skip the state of the game at the close of each head."

LAW XVI.—CHANGING BOWLS

No player shall be allowed to change his bowls in the course of a game unless objected to, as provided in Law II., 2.

LAW XVII.—OBJECTS ON THE GREEN

In a rink game, in no circumstances is any object to be laid on the green, or on a bowl, or on the jack; but it may be displayed in the hand for the guidance of the player. It must, however, be withdrawn immediately the player delivers his bowl.

LAW XVIII.—LEAVING THE GREEN

No player shall be allowed to delay the play by leaving the rink or otherwise unless with the consent of his opponent, and then only for a limited period—not exceeding ten minutes. Contravention of this law will entitle the opposing side to claim the tie.

LAW XIX.—SINGLE-HANDED GAMES

The foregoing Laws, where applicable, shall apply to single-handed and pairs games.

LAW XX.—ONLOOKERS

Persons not engaged in the game must confine themselves to the banks outside the boundaries of the rink, and preserve an attitude of strict neutrality.

> *N.B.*—Audible comment on or criticism of the play and players is in exceedingly bad taste. In the interests of the pastime and its popularity, spectators should be encouraged to attend matches, especially when they are likely to see a fine exposition of the game. But they must refrain from all conduct calculated to annoy Bowlers and perhaps put them off their play.

APPENDIX

INTERNATIONAL RESULTS, 1903 TO 1922, IN ORDER OF MERIT

Two points allotted for a win. In 1903 England v. Scotland tied at 73 all. There has been no other case of a draw.

Country.	Won.	Lost.	Shots. For.	Shots. Against.	Margin.	Points.
1903.						
England . .	2	0	258	196	+ 62	5
Scotland . .	2	0	239	195	+ 44	5
Ireland . .	1	2	209	220	− 11	2
Wales . .	0	3	181	276	− 95	0
1904.						
Scotland . .	3	0	275	200	+ 75	6
England . .	2	1	265	215	+ 50	4
Ireland . .	1	2	213	247	− 34	2
Wales . .	0	3	195	286	− 91	0
1905.						
Ireland . .	2	1	244	219	+ 25	4
Scotland . .	2	1	245	228	+ 17	4
England . .	1	2	232	213	+ 19	2
Wales . .	1	2	201	262	− 61	2
1906.						
England . .	3	0	262	209	+ 53	6
Scotland . .	2	1	237	220	+ 17	4
Wales . .	1	2	212	245	− 33	2
Ireland . .	0	3	204	241	− 37	0
1907.						
Scotland . .	3	0	273	181	+ 92	6
Ireland . .	2	1	254	216	+ 38	4
England . .	1	2	221	252	− 31	2
Wales . .	0	3	189	288	− 99	0

APPENDIX

INTERNATIONAL RESULTS—*continued*

Country.	Won.	Lost.	Shots. For.	Shots. Against.	Margin.	Points.
1908.						
Scotland	2	1	253	214	+ 39	4
Wales	2	1	234	240	− 6	4
England	1	2	224	236	− 12	2
Ireland	1	2	218	239	− 21	2
1909.						
Scotland	3	0	327	191	+136	6
Wales	1	2	234	264	− 30	2
England	1	2	217	265	− 48	2
Ireland	1	2	212	270	− 58	2
1910.						
Scotland	3	0	288	182	+106	6
Ireland	2	1	242	211	+ 31	4
England	1	2	209	265	− 56	2
Wales	0	3	190	271	− 81	0
1911.						
England	3	0	230	199	+ 31	6
Wales	2	1	228	207	+ 21	4
Scotland	1	2	222	239	− 17	2
Ireland	0	3	213	248	− 35	0
1912.						
Scotland	2	1	252	203	+ 49	4
Ireland	2	1	251	233	+ 18	4
England	1	2	220	249	− 29	2
Wales	1	2	209	247	− 38	2

THE INTERNATIONALS

INTERNATIONAL RESULTS—*continued*

Country.	Won.	Lost.	Shots. For.	Shots. Against.	Margin.	Points.
1913.						
Scotland	3	0	271	213	+ 58	6
Wales	2	1	225	224	+ 1	4
Ireland	1	2	225	244	− 19	2
England	0	3	212	252	− 40	0
1914.						
Scotland	2	1	248	213	+ 35	4
Ireland	2	1	240	232	+ 8	4
Wales	1	2	236	255	− 19	2
England	1	2	220	244	− 24	2
1919.						
Scotland	3	0	344	240	+104	6
England	2	1	288	303	− 15	4
Wales	1	2	282	268	+ 14	2
Ireland	0	3	252	355	−103	0
1920.						
Wales	3	0	326	236	+ 90	6
England	2	1	267	306	− 39	4
Scotland	1	2	292	280	+ 12	2
Ireland	0	3	241	304	− 63	0
1921:						
Scotland	3	0	325	241	+ 84	6
Wales	2	1	302	294	+ 8	4
England	1	2	297	303	− 6	2
Ireland	0	3	239	325	− 86	0
1922.						
Scotland	3	0	311	273	+ 38	6
Ireland	2	1	286	262	+ 24	4
Wales	1	2	254	293	− 39	2
England	0	3	260	283	− 23	0

APPENDIX

INTERNATIONAL RESULTS—*continued*

AUSTRALIANS IN BRITAIN

1901	{ Australia { Britain	. . .	1890 1856
1912	{ Australia { Britain	. . .	4599 4330
1922	{ Britain { Australia	. . .	4530 4495

NEW ZEALANDERS IN BRITAIN

1907	{ New Zealand { Scotland	. . .	243 242
1921	{ New Zealand { Britain	. . .	6388 6099

CANADIANS IN BRITAIN

1904	{ Britain { Canada	. . .	3166 2321
1908	{ Britain { Canada	. . .	2975 2506
1913	{ Canada { Britain	. . .	1201 1200

BRITISH IN CANADA

1906	{ Britain { Canada	. . .	3965 2878
1910	{ Britain { Canada	. . .	1924 1645
1921	{ Britain { Canada	. . .	3877 3619

INDEX

Absentee players, law as to, 101.
Alloa, match in winter at, 1.
Attitude in play, 52–3.
Australians in Britain, 115.
Ayres, Messrs. F. H., Bowling green Bowl-makers, 27.

Backhand play, nature of, 47; importance of, 50–1.
Barclay and Perkins's ancient Bowls, 26.
Beginners, advice to, 36–58.
"Be up!" 57.
Bias: definition of, 25; how obtained, 25; abuses of, 31; English B.A.'s investigation, 32; of a standard No. 3, 33; forehand and backhand play, 47–51; against the, 49; law as to, 96; altered, 98.
Bowl, the: described, 24; "biassed," 25; manufacture of, 28–33; dressed with ronuk, 31; under-sized, 33; weight and size prescribed, 35; buying the, 35; how to hold, 56; measuring, 72; law as to size and bias, 96; and as to testing, 97; played by mistake, law as to, 101; and as to change of, during game, 101; law as to a "dead," 105; and rebounding, 106; and burned, 107–8; and as to measurement, 111.
Bowling Club, how to start a, 3–5.
Bowls, advice to a beginner, 36–58; law as to conditions of a match or game at, 99.

British bowlers in Canada, 115.
"Burned" bowl, law as to, 107–8.
"Burned" jack, law as to, 106–7.

Canadians in Britain, 115.
Captain, the, office of, 77.
Carruthers, James Gillespie, both lead and skip, 68; as player, 55.
Chapman, J. R., as lead, 52.
Coach, groundman as, 20; friend should act as, to beginner, 36.
Crown-green game, the, 17–8.

Darwin, Charles, on the *Action of Worms*, 12.
Defaulters, law as to, 101.
Delivery, art of, 51, 54–7.
Ditch, the, 6, 76.
Ditchboard inquiry, the, 6.
Ditchers, 73; law as to, 110.
Drawing in Points game, 80.
Drive, the bowl in, 56; by the skip, 69; the wanton, 76.
Driving [in Points], 86.
Dumping, evils of, 55–6.
Dunciad, The, quoted, 25.

Emmerson, J. S., as player, 52.
Excelite bowl, the, 24.
Expletives, use of, 37.

Firing, on, 70; indiscriminate, 76.
Fixed Jack, game of, 87; preparing the green, 88; the game described, 88; jacks of varying length, 90.
Footer, *see* Mat.

INDEX

Forehand and backhand play, 47, 50–1.

Game, law as to conditions of a, 99.
Gravel, its effect on the bowl, 7.
Green: the ideal, 3; dimensions, 4; the ditch, 6; when to lay a new, 8; weeding, 9; mowing and rolling, 14; level *versus* crown, 17; the ranger or rota, 21; loan of, 22; effect of weather on, 47; after rain, 56; law as to objects on, 111.
Greenkeeper, *see* Groundman.
Greens, "tricky," 15.
Groundman, the, his essential qualifications, 19; in winter, 20; tipping, 21.
Guaiacum officinale, 27.
Guarding, the question of, 71; in Points game, 82.

Hand, position in delivery, 55.
Head, law as to result of, 111.
Hunt, Leigh, on swearing, 36.

International results, 1903–22, 115.

Jack, the: tossing for, 38; who should throw, 38; a minimum and maximum jack, 40; wide of median line, 41–2; an indolent custom, 44; random throwing, 45; names for, 45; effect of weak play to, 57; "live jack," 75–6; law as to size of, 99; and as to throwing, 104; and as to jack driven into ditch, 104; and when "dead," 105; laws as to rebounding, 106; and burned, 106–7.
Johnson, Dr., quoted, 26.

Kew Gardens, lawns at, 10; *lignum vitæ*, sections of, exhibited at, 27.
"Kitty," synonym for jack, 45.

Lawn-mower, use of, 14.

Laws of Bowls, 95–112.
Lead used to give bias, 25.
Leader, the duties of, 61.
Leslie, Daniel, on treatment of greens, 11–12.
Level-green game, the, 1–23.
Lignum vitæ, 27.
Lutton Place green, Edinburgh, 6.

Markers, law as to, 98.
Mat, placing of, 39; law as to position and size, 103.
Measurement of bowls, 72.
Mitchell, William W., plays on Christmas Day, 1879, 2; quoted, 67, 74.

New English Dictionary, quoted, 24–5.
New Zealanders in Britain, 115.

Onlookers, law as to, 112.

Pin, or iron peg, 95.
Playing out of turn, law as to, 101.
Points, game of, 79; the four shots: Drawing, 80; Guarding, 82; Trailing, 84; Driving, 86.
Pope, Alexander, quoted, 25.

Rae, Sir Alexander, on the greens of Wick, 13.
Ranger of the green, 21.
Recorde, Robert, quoted, 26.
Rink, the: definitions of, 59; the Rink Game described, 59–77; law as to team of players, 100; and as to failure of, to appear, 101.
Rinks of the green, law as to, 95; law as to possession of, 110.
Roller, weight of, 14.
Ronuk, for dressing bowls, 31.
Rota, green, 21.

Score, law as to keeping, 111.
Scottish Bowling Association, laws drafted by, 95–111.

INDEX

Scythe, use of, 14.
Second player, the : his importance, 62 ; as scorer, 64.
Shatford, Frank, as Bowler, 52.
Shoes, rubber-soled, imperative, 22.
Skip: the vain, 38; the director, 60 ; and the second player, 63 ; has powers of an autocrat, 66 ; but must be a diplomatist, 67 ; a tactician, 68 ; the ideal skip, 69 ; as driver, 69 ; firing, 70 ; what may be his last duty, 71 ; how to win and lose, 72 ; law as to duties of, 102.
Solway turf, 8.
Spittle, a mark of honour, 74.
Style, its attractiveness, 51.

"Take Green !" 58.
Testing a bowl, law as to, 97.
Third man, skip's deputy, 65 ; measurement taken by, 72.

Tie, law as to, 99.
Tossing, law as to, for jack, 100.
Touchers, 71 ; definition of, 73 ; law as to, 109.
Trailing in Points game, 84.
Turf, various points to be considered, 1–23.
Turner, M., of Carlisle Subscription B.C., 52.

Unwritten law, 18.

Visualising the track of bowl, 47, 52.

Weeds, to eradicate, 10.
Weight of bowl, 31, 35.
Wick, Bowls in, 13.
Windrim, Samuel, of Shaftesbury B.C., Belfast, 52.
Winter play at Bowls, 2.
Worms, their action, 12 ; an effective killer, 13.

www.ingramcontent.com/pod-product-compliance
Lightning Source LLC
Chambersburg PA
CBHW030235170426
43201CB00006B/226